About Island Press

Since 1984, the nonprofit organization Island Press has been stimulating, shaping, and communicating ideas that are essential for solving environmental problems worldwide. With more than 1,000 titles in print and some 30 new releases each year, we are the nation's leading publisher on environmental issues. We identify innovative thinkers and emerging trends in the environmental field. We work with world-renowned experts and authors to develop cross-disciplinary solutions to environmental challenges.

Island Press designs and executes educational campaigns, in conjunction with our authors, to communicate their critical messages in print, in person, and online using the latest technologies, innovative programs, and the media. Our goal is to reach targeted audiences—scientists, policy makers, environmental advocates, urban planners, the media, and concerned citizens—with information that can be used to create the framework for long-term ecological health and human well-being.

Island Press gratefully acknowledges major support from The Bobolink Foundation, Caldera Foundation, The Curtis and Edith Munson Foundation, The Forrest C. and Frances H. Lattner Foundation, The JPB Foundation, The Kresge Foundation, The Summit Charitable Foundation, Inc., and many other generous organizations and individuals.

The opinions expressed in this book are those of the author(s) and do not necessarily reflect the views of our supporters.

A HEALTHY UNION

A HEALTHY UNION

How States Can Lead on Environmental Health

SUSAN BETH KAPLAN

ISLANDPRESS

Washington | Covelo

Library of Congress Control Number: 2025935892

All Island Press books are printed on environmentally responsible materials.

Manufactured in the United States of America
10 9 8 7 6 5 4 3 2 1

KEYWORDS: California AB 617; Centers of Excellence in Children's Environmental Health; Chemical exposure; Children's health; Environmental and occupational health education; Environmental health policy; Environmental justice; Health in All Policies; Massachusetts Toxics Use Reduction Act; Minnesota Toxic Free Kids Act; Occupational Health Clinic Network; Pesticide drift; PFAS; Public health; Regional Greenhouse Gas Initiative; Southeast Regional Partnership for Planning and Sustainability; Tennessee Livability Collaborative; Toxics

MIX
Paper | Supporting responsible forestry
FSC® C005010
FSC www.fsc.org

For David, Benji, and Welcome

And for Romeo,
who snoozed warmly beside me the whole time

CONTENTS

Introduction

CREATING HEALTHY ENVIRONMENTS

When my older son was two years old, our family moved to a small city that boasts a reputation as politically and environmentally progressive. It is located in a state that not long ago shifted from "red" to "blue."[1] So I was taken aback when, that first May, ChemLawn trucks and landscapers clustered in the streets, spraying weedkiller from backpack containers, thick hoses, and even a tractor, leaving little white flags planted in the bright green golf course–like grass and a strong chemical odor in the air. This included not only neighbors' yards but the massive lawn of the retirement home that occupied a full square block, just yards from the elementary school my children would attend.

I was surprised and concerned—and, after my son was diagnosed with asthma a few years later, alarmed. As an environmental health lawyer and professor, I knew that children are especially vulnerable to toxic exposures. Their cells are dividing rapidly, they breathe more air relative to their body weight than adults, and their immature organs are unable to excrete and detoxify harmful substances as well as adults'. Even low-level toxic exposures can cause them long-term or even permanent harm. Herbicides are linked with asthma exacerbation and onset, Parkinson's disease, reproductive problems, and more. When sprayed, they can drift through the air and be inhaled. They can also be absorbed through the skin (and ingested, in the case of food).

I had assumed that this well-educated, liberal town had policies that would protect my son and that my neighbors were well familiar with the issue. But during the years of advocacy that followed, I began to understand why this wasn't the case. Like forty-plus others, the state has a law limiting local pesticide policies. Its economy is largely agricultural and chemical-intensive. There were few pesticide-reduction policies in the region, lessening knowledge of best practices. I found that a slice of the community was environmentally aware, while the overall culture was not. All these factors overlapped and fed into each other.

With the federal government politically divided nearly to the point of immobilization in recent years, most environmental health protections take place (or don't) on the state level, and sometimes on the local level. As a professional and a parent, this is where my journey began.

❧

In many parts of this country, a child could go to gym class on a typical Monday and play soccer on a field that was sprayed over the weekend with 2,4-D, a weedkiller that was a component of Agent Orange and has been investigated as possibly causing cancer.[2] Or the school grounds may have been treated with a lower-toxicity herbicide, or with safe, nontoxic products and practices. Which of these scenarios applies depends largely on the laws of the child's state of residence; federal law provides only bare-bones protection. State policies can affect community members' exposure to air pollution and to toxic chemicals like per- and polyfluoroalkyl substances, or PFAS—a group of synthetic substances that are added to items to make them oil-, stain-, or water-resistant—and flame retardants, and even whether a product label must list these. While states can be valuable laboratories of innovation, major differences in environmental health laws contribute to inequities in pollution exposures—and, data suggest, health outcomes.

Environmental health (sometimes referred to as environmental public health) is defined by the National Environmental Health Association as "the science and practice of preventing human injury and illness and promoting well-being by identifying and evaluating environmental sources and hazardous agents; and limiting exposures to hazardous physical, chemical, and biological agents in air, water, soil, food, and other environmental media or settings that may adversely affect human health."[3] It pertains to involuntary exposures—so unhappily breathing secondhand smoke as a patron in a hotel bar is an environmental health issue, while smoking, as a personal choice, is not.

Doug Farquhar, government affairs director for the National Environmental Health Association, writes that environmental health law is a "novel concept" in that it incorporates "both society's public health needs" and the environmental factors that affect it. He notes that most major environmental laws are in fact environmental health laws, since they identify protection of public health "as a major justification" for the law.[4] Yet environmental health is typically a lesser-known part of public health than spheres like health care access.

When it comes to limiting people's exposure to pollution and toxins, state policies have taken precedence as the federal government has increasingly retreated from major environmental health lawmaking. As I wrote in an article for *The Conversation*:

> Many of the country's major environmental health laws were passed in the 1970s on the momentum of the environmental movement and with bipartisan support that is rarely seen today.
>
> For example, the Clean Air Act amendments of 1970 required U.S. EPA to regulate a wide range of air pollutants, in some cases based explicitly on protecting human health. They were approved 374–1 in the House and 73–0 by the Senate and signed into law by President Richard M. Nixon. Nixon signed the law that created the Occupational Safety and Health Administration in 1971.
>
> One analyst has written that groups that pressed legislators for environmental protection later splintered into groups advocating for and against environmental laws, reflecting an emerging debate over the appropriate extent of regulation.
>
> At the same time, after the success of many federal environmental health laws, attention turned to problems that are harder for Washington to solve. With state environmental programs growing, some suggested that the U.S. EPA's role should shift from compelling to catalyzing—from requiring specific pollution-reducing actions to helping states act by providing increased information and help with compliance. Yet this view acknowledged that under this scenario, residents of some states would enjoy stronger environmental health protections than others.

Reflecting this dynamic and the extent of political division in the U.S., even when the federal government does create tougher environmental regulations, they are often reversed by the succeeding administration or challenged in court.[5]

Most Americans—even knowledgeable professionals—assume that when they go to the grocery or hardware store or drop their child off at school, the government has ensured the safety of all products and practices in those places. In fact, due to major policy gaps at the federal level, if a state has not addressed an environmental health issue, then it may be unaddressed.

Sometimes it makes sense for states to take the lead in policymaking. Different states face differing environmental health challenges, from hurricanes to flooding to wildfires to varying sorts of pests and pollution. States may have different politics, priorities, climates, and cultures. States have always had an important role as laboratories of innovation. Policies tested out at the state level can help to inform decisions of other states and of the federal government.

But uneven environmental health protections create inequities. For example, those who reside in a state that follows California's more stringent tailpipe emissions standards—about one-third of the states—probably benefit from breathing less air pollution from that source. The Regional Greenhouse Gas Initiative (RGGI) is another state-based innovation. It limits greenhouse gas emissions in participating states, which results in reducing other harmful air pollutants too. A recent study that compared RGGI states with neighboring states that have not signed on to RGGI found that data "indicate that RGGI has provided substantial child health benefits," including a reduction in childhood asthma cases.[6]

There are many more examples. Minnesota's Toxic Free Kids Act requires the health department to develop a list of chemicals of concern for children's health and communicate the risks; several others have similar laws. States have passed a patchwork of limits on PFAS in products. Providing water- and stain-resistance to everything from fabrics to nonstick cookware, PFAS are known as "forever chemicals" because of their persistence in the environment and have recently been linked with a range of troubling health effects.[7]

These policy questions about the role of federal and state governments matter now, not only because of unprecedented environmental health challenges like climate change–worsened heat and smog and expanded travel of pests carrying infectious diseases, and everyday toxic chemical exposures— but because the increasing impacts on vulnerable groups can have lifelong ramifications. Children exposed to carcinogenic chemicals have many years ahead in which to develop cancer; seventy-year-olds have far fewer. When lead, mercury, or pesticide exposure contributes to a child's autism or ADHD, those conditions may require specialized education and limit their career options and lifetime earnings. When a fourth grader with asthma breathes a disinfectant cleaner like bleach, they are more likely to wheeze than someone who does not already have that disease; they have been sensitized. When a resident of an environmental justice community encounters heavy truck exhaust while walking to the bus stop due to siting of a new fulfillment warehouse nearby, that toxic diesel exhaust may augment existing air pollution common to such neighborhoods and contribute to more severe lung inflammation.

Overall, broader, better federal environmental health protections are ideal and should be the overarching goal. But in their absence, states should act. Where it truly makes sense for states to take the lead—as in the case of COVID-19—the federal government must provide comprehensive, clear, easy-to-access data, information, and guidance to states and localities.

✐

This book begins by examining historic and structural contributors to the quandary of federal shortcomings in environmental health regulation. It describes how states began to act to fill these gaps, the challenges they have encountered along the way, and the uneven results and inequities created or exacerbated, along with best-practice models that other states have replicated or signed on to.

Next, the book explores strategies for success, reflected in the enactment and implementation of innovative state policies—as well as an example of strategies that were needed but were absent or stymied for a variety of reasons. The strategies are as follows:

- State-university-industry partnerships and technical assistance, as exemplified by the Massachusetts Toxics Use Reduction Act and Texas's law requiring pesticide reduction policies and practices in all schools

- Environmental and occupational health education, modeled by New York State's Occupational Health Clinic Network and Centers of Excellence in Children's Environmental Health
- Community action, exemplified by California's AB 617 law, the Community Air Protection Program, which aims to improve air quality and advance environmental justice in the state
- Collaboration across agencies, often referred to as a Health in All Policies approach, with the Tennessee Livability Collaborative and Colorado's Health in All Policies program as prototypes
- The need for federal guidance, with COVID-19 mitigation in schools as an example of a situation in which states bear responsibility but the federal government must provide data and guidance in order for states to be successful
- Cooperation across states, like the Regional Greenhouse Gas Initiative of Northeastern and mid-Atlantic states, and the Southeast Regional Partnership for Planning and Sustainability that includes federal agencies and states located in the Southeast, as examples of partnering to cut greenhouse gases and strengthen environmental security at the regional level

Finally, this book identifies policy goals that can help make our communities, states, and nation healthier. And it recommends actions that public health professionals and others can take to advance these policy goals and therefore environmental health protections across all states. It describes strategies for advocating for environmental health policies to officials from school board members to state agency decision-makers.

A growing number of public health professionals are seeking this background to navigate their work. Yet as they face these increasing demands, they are challenged by chronically reduced agency funding and staffing, per the cycle of "panic and neglect" in which governments give attention and funding to a new public health threat, only to withdraw it once the immediate crisis abates;[8] the politicization of public health since COVID-19, along with, in some states, the loss of local public health officials' authority by state legislatures that have preempted it; and concern about a lack of new federal environmental health laws that could help to guide state and local efforts.

Whether navigating issues like the enormous range of health impacts of climate change or protecting "fence-line" communities adjacent to polluting facilities, public health professionals want to understand the policy terrain and take action. Academics want their research findings to reach policymakers. Medical and public health associations are offering trainings on the legislative process and how professionals can make themselves heard within it. This is a critical time for the role of state and local environmental public health. This book aims to provide information and analysis that can further these efforts, ensuring better health for all of our kids.

ONE

A Lack of Federal Protections

The first questions I explored in seeking a solution to the pesticide problem were the following: How does the US Environmental Protection Agency (EPA)—the federal agency that sits atop the environmental health regulatory pyramid—address pesticide use on and around school grounds? How helpful is the main federal law—the Federal Insecticide, Fungicide, and Rodenticide Act (FIFRA)—in protecting my son from toxic weedkillers and insecticides on the playground and soccer field and while riding his bike around the neighborhood?

EPA registers pesticide products for use based on a finding that they do not cause an "unreasonable" risk. Under the law, this determination requires a cost-benefit analysis that takes into account "the economic, social, and environmental costs and benefits" of the use of the pesticide,[1] which can include costs to industry of being prevented from using a pesticide. As a result of this and other influences, many agricultural pesticides that are banned or being phased out in other countries are still widely used in the United States.[2]

Many of FIFRA's requirements for proper use, along with safety information, reside on the product label. Among its other shortcomings, the label may omit ingredients considered trade secrets.[3] In the fable of the label, school and municipal administrators properly interpret its cryptic scientific and regulatory terms and make informed decisions in selecting safer products. Or, as the label fairy tale unfolds, they know to access and understand the more detailed Safety Data Sheet (SDS). Typical SDSs are long—

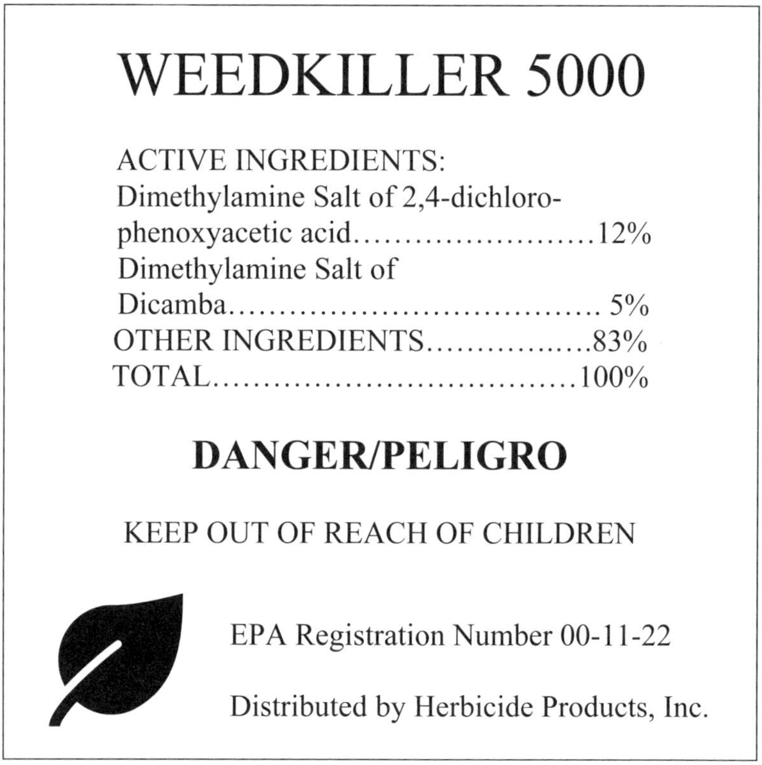

WEEDKILLER 5000

ACTIVE INGREDIENTS:
Dimethylamine Salt of 2,4-dichloro-
phenoxyacetic acid........................12%
Dimethylamine Salt of
Dicamba.................................... 5%
OTHER INGREDIENTS................83%
TOTAL....................................100%

DANGER/PELIGRO

KEEP OUT OF REACH OF CHILDREN

EPA Registration Number 00-11-22

Distributed by Herbicide Products, Inc.

FIGURE 1-1. Example herbicide label

often eight to ten pages—and full of gaps, reflecting how much is unknown about these chemicals.

For example, the simplified example herbicide label shown in Figure 1-1 is typical in that more than half of the product's ingredients ("other ingredients," sometimes referred to as "inert") are not identified. The word "Danger" on the label carries distinct regulatory significance, but few people will be familiar with that meaning—including many school building and grounds managers who make decisions about purchase and use of these products.

Another shortcoming: Neither EPA nor FIFRA impose any requirements beyond the restrictions on the label for states, local governments, park districts, or school districts to develop pesticide use plans, or to limit pesticide use, including in or around environments sheltering sensitive groups, such as schools, daycares, and hospitals.

EPA does provide high-quality resources, such as model sustainable pest control policies. In the absence of a state requirement or state outreach, however, it is uncertain what would inspire a municipality or school district to seek out these resources. Taking such initiative would likely require the awareness and concern of a staff person or parent, perhaps combined with an advocacy effort seeking a change in practices.

Such deficiencies are not unusual. Many federal environmental health laws contain shortfalls and loopholes—for example, putting the (difficult to surmount) burden of proof on the government to show that a substance is harmful, or considering exposure to only a single substance rather than the more realistic multiple simultaneous exposures, or requiring an economic analysis that sidelines public health costs and benefits. The extent of these gaps can be surprising. An October 2023 *New York Times* article that described California's move to ban red food dye, while the Food and Drug Administration had not, quoted one lobbyist for the law, "Many people were astounded to learn that the F.D.A. is not actively regulating the chemicals we put in our food."[4] In February 2024, media described how lead-tainted applesauce had "sailed through" gaps in the federal food safety system.[5] In the patchwork federal environmental health regulatory system, the government fails to address important issues in regulating toxic substances.

How did this situation come to be?

FEDERAL SHIFTS LEAD TO FRAGMENTATION

Analysts including Paul Knechtges of East Carolina University describe a split that goes back to the early 1900s, when the environmental movement divided into natural resources conservation, on one hand, and sanitary improvements in cities, on the other. Naturalists expanded the environmental movement via the growing role of the federal government in managing natural resources during the Progressive Era, Knechtges writes. By contrast, "the sanitary improvement efforts were more diffuse; they were spread across major municipalities rather than being consolidated under federal mandates."[6]

Same roots, different shoots: Environmental activism took off through the 1970s and beyond, while public health failed to develop a broad-based movement. Public health organizations thus found themselves "on the periphery" of the environmental movement, writes Knechtges. The passage of one major federal environmental law after another "would entrench separation of various environmental public health services."[7]

Major structural shifts took place at the federal level when the EPA was established in 1970, at the start of the "Environmental Decade." Many environmental health programs that addressed the health impacts of environmental conditions (such as drinking water quality and air pollution control), previously based in other federal agencies, were moved to EPA. The aim was to "unify" the path to environmental protection, says Thomas Burke of Johns Hopkins University's public health school.[8] Instead, this move caused "fragmented responsibility, lack of coordination, and inadequate attention to public health dimensions of environmental issues," according to the National Academy of Medicine (formerly the Institute of Medicine).[9]

Additionally, the transposition of environmental health programs to EPA was then "replicated at the state levels,"[10] writes Johns Hopkins University public health professor Beth Resnick. Just as at the federal level, the states also moved environmental programs out of their health departments, which had traditionally led programs like drinking water quality, says Burke. As a result, "we got a really balkanized system."[11] Environmental health programs and policies are now often housed in departments such as environment and natural resources, with a smattering assigned to agriculture, labor, and health agencies.

The conundrum: State environment and natural resource agencies that took on tasks previously assigned to public health agencies may lack expertise in health impacts of environmental decisions. At the same time, state and local public health agencies may lack training about—and give insufficient attention to—environmental influences on health. This fragmentation of environmental health can mean that an environmental agency might not prioritize health aspects of its work, while a public health agency underemphasizes impacts of pollution and toxics on health. The fragmentation can cause an overall siloing effect in which environmental issues and public health issues are addressed separately by separate agencies and staff, leaving critical problems that overlap the two areas ungrappled with.

Decades beyond the 1970s, this "splintering of environmental public health functions still exists today in most states," notes Knechtges."[12] In a 1997 study of state government environmental health infrastructure, Thomas Burke, Nadia Shalauta, Nga Tran, and Barry S. Stern found great diversity in the organization of environmental health programs. In surveying the state agencies that implement ten federal environmental laws, including the Clean Air Act, Clean Water Act, and laws addressing hazardous materials, the study authors noted that while these laws may have strengthened state capabilities, they may also have "forced a narrower state focus toward the regulatory aspects of environmental protection and away from the broader public health aspects."[13]

Emphasizing federal requirements to manage air and water pollution and waste management and having grown dependent on federal funding for these activities, state environmental agencies lack capabilities in epidemiology and risk assessment that enable an understanding of health impacts of environmental conditions—one side of the disconnect. On the other side of the disconnect, the study found that health departments continue to have primary responsibility for the public health aspects of environmental programs—health assessment, toxics programs, health surveillance, and environmental epidemiology—but with little regulatory authority for these programs. Additionally, the authors note that state budgets for environmental regulatory programs were four times greater than those for environmental health programs.

While Burke and colleagues note that the growth and diversification of environmental programs is positive, the main question is whether staff working in these two areas of environmental protection and public health are able to reach past silos and work together to maximize environmental health protection.

Another challenge is data and data integration. According to Megan Wallace and Joshua M. Sharfstein of Johns Hopkins University's public health school, while public health relies on information technology and data, "much of state and local public health work remains based on paper, with large gaps in the ability of health departments to obtain, analyze, and share information expeditiously."[14] Additionally, they find that over one-third of local health departments cannot access electronic data from local emergency departments that "could facilitate early identification of illnesses of concern." Therefore, a spike in children's visits to emergency departments for asthma attacks may be unknown to the local public health director, who in an ideal world is on the ground connecting asthma emergencies with contributors such as air pollution and toxics.

Consider that even before my son's asthma was diagnosed, I had observed that many of his friends and classmates had this illness. In fact, based on my nonscientific observations, I guessed that about 25 percent of the kids at his elementary school suffered from this breathing disorder. By any measure, that appears to be an epidemic—or some might say a cluster, which implies group proximity to an environmental trigger that is causing or contributing to a disease. Some might say that it qualifies as an emergency.

I worried my son was next, and I was right—along with his pal who lived two blocks from us and was diagnosed within weeks of him. Yet no one commented on or seemed to recognize a pattern. Where was the incidence data, the understanding of environmental triggers of asthma and how to reduce them, the knowledge about how to identify such pollution sources in the neighborhood? Some data about the extent of the problem likely resided in the school nurse's files. Other pieces of the puzzle may have been held by staff of different agencies—or not, due to deficiencies in education, training, staffing, data, or technology. The pieces were never put together.

What might a collaborative approach look like? Maybe like this: The state or local health department conducts surveillance that identifies an asthma hot spot in a community—25 percent of children in that area, let's say, have been diagnosed with the disease—then partners with environmental agency staff to identify indoor or outdoor asthma triggers, increase education and enforcement, and develop new policies to reduce instigators of asthma problems. They bring in other agencies and organizations as called for, such as the school district and park district. This de-siloed approach is more likely to improve environmental health outcomes in terms of reduced asthma diagnoses and exacerbations than an incomplete, siloed approach that only views and addresses one patch of the quilt.

Or consider high-volume hydraulic horizontal fracturing, or fracking, a process in which a mixture of sand, water, and chemicals is injected deep underground to break up shale rock and release natural gas for energy use. Fracking has raised public health concerns due to the many trucks (and their diesel exhaust) used to transport materials to and from the sites; the potential for exposure to toxic chemicals (benzene and many others) via inhalation or due to leaks and spills of wastewater; and possible contamination of groundwater after the fracking operation is completed. The operation is frequently carried out near residences and schools, meaning children and other vulnerable groups can be exposed to these risks.

Fracking is exempt from the federal Safe Drinking Water Act due to the "Halliburton loophole," named for the company that former Vice President

Dick Cheney headed. So the issue moves to the states, which may have varying views of fracking's appeal given their economic, environmental, social, and other priorities. Consider a situation in which a state legislature passes a law allowing fracking, then delegates development of regulations, which flesh out the law, to the state's natural resources agency. Its staff may competently manage decisions affecting land and minerals, but do they have the capability to incorporate consideration of potential health impacts on nearby residents in their analysis? If not, are they partnering with sister agencies that do possess that expertise? Who is protecting environmental health?

Given the regulatory gaps at the federal level, many environmental health issues are addressed—*if* they are addressed—at the state and local levels. But they often are not. Given expansive and growing daily challenges like addressing the many impacts of climate change and the spread of toxic chemicals, significantly more collaboration among state agency functions is needed.

INDUSTRY INFLUENCE

A major contributor to environmental health regulatory gaps is the influence of industry. Industry associations' bedrock near K Street and the US Capitol lessens into a smaller flow beyond the Beltway as it migrates to statehouses and occasionally city hall. Industry mechanisms of influence are well-oiled and well-established and often outweigh the will of regular citizens. *Roll Call* reports that the ten highest spenders on lobbying laid out $326.6 million in 2022 in an effort to press the federal government to favor their positions.[15] On the one hand, when it comes to worker safety and health regulatory development, the national labor unions, with their offices encircling the Department of Labor, enjoy proximity and connections. But it is more challenging for consumers to serve as an effective counterweight to the National Association of Manufacturers, American Chemistry Council, American Petroleum Institute, and US Chamber of Commerce. There is no one organization or constituency representing US consumers or parents.

Modes of industry influence include involvement developing laws and regulations, filing lawsuits to impel changes, funding research studies, and making cash contributions to politicians who are in a decision-making position. As far as impacts on research, the authors of an article in *BioScience* express concern that the EPA's risk-assessment process for pesticides and other chemicals "can proceed using a narrow portion of the available data and can be based exclusively on industry-supplied studies . . . which has inherent conflicts of interest."[16] The authors, led by Michelle D. Boone of Miami University and Christine A. Bishop of Environment Canada, write that such conflicts of interest are "ingrained in the process," in part because EPA works hand in hand with industry to establish study methodology, which can be "prohibitively expensive for researchers outside of industry." Therefore, much or even all of the data that EPA considers as part of risk assessments may come from research carried out or funded by industry, "despite clear conflicts of interest." The authors also cite research finding that studies submitted to regulatory agencies by industry are more likely to support findings favorable to industry.[17]

In terms of lobbying power, after California passed its innovative Proposition 65 law, which limits water pollution emissions and requires warning labels for chemicals that cause cancer or birth defects, other states tried to follow its example. But opponents, who hadn't expected Prop 65 to succeed, "crushed" those efforts with "massively funded political campaigns," according to a Stanford Law School blog.[18] Burke of Johns Hopkins notes that New Jersey made early, critical strides in developing programs that led to federal laws like Superfund. It created a unique right-to-know law to provide hazard information to both workers and communities. But that was "before the rise of the trade associations," Burke says. "They made enormous campaign contributions to politicians to prevent action and worked to 'manufacture doubt'"—referring to industry efforts to create uncertainty about harms like smoking and climate change.

Some recent industry efforts have focused on preemption—when a higher level of government prevents or limits a lower level of government from regulating a particular issue. This has been more commonplace in statehouses, where lawmakers may preempt the ability of local governments in that state to address an environmental health concern. According to the US Centers for Disease Control and Prevention (CDC), ceiling preemption, which prevents local governments from establishing more stringent ordinances than those established by state law, has become "almost routine" in legislative and regulatory processes recently, especially on issues involving health protection and consumer protection.[19] For example, due to a concerted industry pressure campaign on statehouses in the 1990s, more than forty states now have laws preempting local governments' ability to regulate pesticide use. State preemption laws are increasing, limiting the regulatory abilities of local governments on issues ranging from minimum wage to firearms. Regenerating the autonomy and power of localities in the face of state preemption efforts is now a major goal within the field of public health.

If challenges like preemption can be addressed, then, given the stagnation at the federal level and the uneven environmental health protections at the state level, city hall can be freed to develop new, innovative policy ideas on a small scale. Sited out of the way, geared to idiosyncratic local issues, the town council is less likely to be pressured by external special interests and more able to act quickly and creatively—which can produce lessons learned that are useful for other localities and for states.

THE END OF FEDERAL ACCORD

A third explanation for the slowing of federal environmental health policy is today's rabid political divisions, which differ from decades ago, when many laws were passed with bipartisan support. Harvard University environmental law professor Richard Lazarus explains that since President George H.W. Bush began to pull back on environmental efforts for political reasons, there has been "presidential administration whiplash" from one regime to the next, and a simultaneous end to new environmental laws coming from Congress. Without the ability to pass new legislation, every administration is trying to tack new goals onto old laws, "which does not easily fit," says Lazarus, and "is a disaster for lawmaking."[20]

Assuming the federal government can remain open for business—shutdowns and threats of shutdowns having become frequent in recent years[21]—bills to protect environmental health typically pass, if they do pass, with an exceedingly narrow margin. The Inflation Reduction Act of 2022, for example, which addressed climate change among other issues, was approved by the House of Representatives 220–207 and the Senate 51–50, entirely along party lines.

Even when the federal government creates tougher environmental laws or regulations, they are often reversed by the succeeding administration or challenged in court. In 2022, the Supreme Court struck down the Clean Power Plan, determining that the EPA lacked authority under the Clean Air Act to regulate greenhouse gas emissions by requiring power plants system-wide to adopt cleaner energy sources.[22] Such an authorization to the EPA would seem to require new climate legislation from Congress—almost unthinkable at present.

Following on that decision, the Supreme Court heard a case challenging the "*Chevron* doctrine," the traditional deference given to federal agencies like EPA when they make a "reasonable interpretation" of an ambiguous law. Such deference has been granted for several decades, on the assumption that an agency's toxicologists, biostatisticians, and other experts are best placed to make such a determination. With the court's 2024 decision to reverse *Chevron* in the case *Loper Bright Enterprises vs. Raimondo*, agencies will no longer enjoy this deference and agency experts may be overruled more often by judges who have less expertise in the area of policy in question. Notably, since the decision applies only to federal agencies, it may further move the main locus of environmental health policymaking to the states.

More broadly, some observers believe that EPA itself has failed to evolve so as to maintain its relevance. Kenneth Olden, former director of both the National Institute of Environmental Health Sciences and National Center for Environmental Assessment, compares EPA with the National Institutes of Health (NIH), asserting that NIH reinvented itself and remained relevant while EPA stagnated.[23] He writes that after EPA succeeded in cleaning up dramatically dirty skies and waterways, many people no longer saw environmental protection as a priority. At that point, he writes, EPA should have made the case that environmental protection is critical over the long term and addresses hazards that can have dire impacts "even though one may not be able to see, taste, or smell them." EPA needed to put "a human face on environmental protection by linking invisible pollutants to human health." EPA also needed to recalibrate to address more scattered sources of pollution, such as farm runoff, he writes. By contrast, he believes that NIH, after accomplishing its original job of stemming the epidemic of infectious diseases, "identified the new scientific challenges associated with the rise in life expectancy," such as chronic disease, and expanded into twenty-plus centers supported by substantial funding (although its budget has since been reduced).

∽

So as outdoor workers grow increasingly weak from heat exhaustion during steamier summers, viruses previously viewed as exotic travel poleward, and consumers seek personal care products free of endocrine-disrupting chemicals, the heavy clouds above leave us vulnerable below, lacking umbrellas and protection. If we want to stay protected, we need to create our own. With federal environmental health protections lessening, state and local guardrails become our refuge for those of us lucky enough to enjoy them. How has this played out?

TWO

Enter the States

Our federalist system assumes that states may do what the federal government doesn't. In some cases, it makes sense to leave decisions to states. They can prioritize issues specific to that geographic area or to more localized preferences. A health department in a Western state may focus on protecting schoolchildren or outdoor workers from wildfire smoke, as this has been a more prevalent problem in that part of the country. Some states may welcome fracking operations while others elect to keep them out. States can serve as laboratories of innovation, testing new policies and programs to see how they work. Those that turn out to be winners may be adapted and adopted by other states, or even by the federal government.

In the absence of federal environmental health standards—or of federal standards adequate to protect human health—states began to act.

STATES START TO FILL THE GAPS

From the start, California blazed its own trail. It was the sole recipient of a waiver under the motor vehicle provisions of the Clean Air Act, allowing it to set its own standards to reduce air pollution from motor vehicles and, therefore, improve public health. Given its economy—so enormous that, as of April 2025, it would be the world's fourth largest if it was a country[1]— and Los Angeles's historically smoggy skies, Congress gave this state the singular authority to set standards that are stricter than federal requirements. While the continuation of the waiver has sometimes been in question in recent years, California's influence in this area remains unchanged.

Its impacts are widespread. California's emission limits have been adopted by seventeen states and the District of Columbia, as shown in the two columns under the heading "LEV regulations" in table 2-1. Yet the exchange of policies works in both directions. California developed the nation's first vehicle emissions standards in 1966, before the federal government developed standards. Two years later, the EPA adopted California's standards for that year's cars. UCLA law professor Ann Carlson calls this pattern, in which California innovates and federal regulators piggyback on the state's demonstrated success, "iterative federalism." This practice has continued for decades.[2]

California's Zero-Emission Vehicle requirement, another piece of its efforts to lower motor vehicle emissions, was enacted in 1990 and has evolved as technological advances have moved transportation in the direction of zero emissions.[3] Most recently, California pushed the environmental health envelope again with its commitment for new vehicles to be zero emission starting in 2035. Charging infrastructure and other elements of ensuring these vehicles are convenient for drivers are also required. Many of the same states have piggybacked on these efforts, too—see column "ZEV program" in table 2-1. (As a note, several aspects of California's vehicle emission programs became uncertain starting in January 2025.)

Other California environmental health innovations exert a similarly outsized influence on the rest of the country. The state's Proposition 65— the Safe Drinking Water and Toxic Enforcement Act of 1986—requires that it develop an updated list of chemicals known to the state to cause cancer or reproductive harms. Businesses must include warning labels on products that contain chemicals on the list. Due to California's size and economic impact, residents of states from Arkansas to Alaska may notice Proposition 65 warnings on their new shirt or at the entrance to the airplane they board. And manufacturers may devise new formulations—free of components on the Proposition 65 list—of a product that is marketed nationally, to ensure they can sell it in California.

At the local level, San Francisco's Integrated Pest Management policy is widely viewed as a national model. It, too, includes a list—the Reduced Risk Pesticide List of products that have undergone the city's own Pesticide Hazard Screening Protocol (and meant for the use of city departments).[4]

TABLE 2-1. States that have adopted California's vehicle emission standards, specifically Low-Emission Vehicle (LEV) criteria pollutant and greenhouse gas emission regulations and Zero-Emission Vehicle (ZEV) regulations, under the Clean Air Act. The table depicts the model year (MY) the state adoptions took/take effect and is current as of May 13, 2022.

| | Applicable model year | | |
| | LEV regulations | | |
State	Criteria pollutant regulation	GHG regulation	ZEV program
California	1992	2009	1990
New York	1993	2009	1993
Massachusetts	1995	2009	1995
Vermont	2000	2009	2000
Maine	2001	2009	2001
Pennsylvania	2001	2009	
Connecticut	2008	2009	2008
Rhode Island	2008	2009	2008
Washington	2009	2009	2025
Oregon	2009	2009	2009
New Jersey	2009	2009	2009
Maryland	2011	2011	2011
Delaware	2014	2014	
Colorado	2022	2022	2023
Minnesota	2025	2025	2025
Nevada	2025	2025	2025
Virginia	2025	2025	2025
New Mexico	2026	2026	2026

(*Source*: California Air Resources Board)

Municipalities around the country reference San Francisco's list in their own pesticide-reduction policies—thereby multiplying its impact—often alongside the EPA's list of safer pesticides.

THE GAP-FILLING IS UNEVEN ACROSS THE STATES

When I observed the high rate of asthma among children in my neighborhood, I was largely on my own in reaching out to local policymakers and experts to express my concerns and request assistance. I also reached out to a state agency. But getting a helpful response was an uphill battle. I made the changes that my son's pediatrician had recommended to address his asthma, which focused on the indoor environment: high-efficiency air filter in his room, pillow and mattress covers to protect against dust mites. But our indoor environment was already pretty allergy- and asthma-safe. After all, I worked professionally in the field of environmental and occupational health. So I started learning about outdoor asthma triggers. And I learned and I learned. There was a lot to know.

Why did this time-consuming (not to mention expensive, given everything I had to buy) burden fall on me? Some states do better than others at filling the environmental health policy gaps left by federal shortcomings. Why? Culture is clearly a factor. Wisconsin, for example, has deep seeds of prioritizing conservation and pollution prevention, planted at least in part by the Scandinavian and German immigrants who brought their progressive beliefs with them from across the ocean. University of Wisconsin professor and ecologist Aldo Leopold wrote about the importance of protecting the land in his influential 1949 book, *A Sand County Almanac*. Wisconsin Senator Gaylord Nelson originated Earth Day. The state has historically made a greater commitment to environmental protection than many others.[5] Massachusetts has, too, likely influenced by the Puritan waste-not ethic and the naturalistic ethos of Henry David Thoreau, both going back to the Bay State's earliest days.[6]

Another influence is the wealth of the state in question; in general, those with more funds spend more on environmental (and, by extension, environmental health) protection.[7]

The dominant contributors to a state's economy matter. Tulane University environmental studies and public policy professor Joshua Basseches and colleagues confirm that enacting climate change–focused laws can be more challenging in states where fossil fuel companies provide jobs and tax revenue.[8] This likely also applies to economic drivers like agriculture or minerals extraction. Basseches et al. also pinpoint the challenge of "fragmentation of pro-climate policy coalitions"—for example, when representatives of the solar power industry jockey for influence with wind power companies, thereby weakening the strength of the renewable power sector as a force when it goes up against organized "powerful fossil fuel incumbents."

Partisan politics matter, too, with Democrats more often casting votes in favor of the environment.[9] But there are important limitations to this generalization. In interviews with state legislators, Vanderbilt University sociology professor David Hess and his colleagues Quan D. Mai and Kate Pride Brown found that framing of bills that advance renewable energy and energy efficiency (which protect environmental health via cleaner air) affected their likelihood of passage. Examining bills proposed between 2004 and 2014, they found that legislators distinguished them based on frames related to ideological differences. When proposed policies were structured as mandates—such as requirements to increase use of renewable energy by a certain percentage—there was less support than for similar policies structured as tax reductions (like tax credits for installing solar power), reduction of government waste by increasing building efficiency, and expansion of the ability of local governments to act.[10]

For example, Hess, Mai, and Brown list laws aimed at increasing building energy efficiency that passed in "red" states. These lean in the direction of goals and incentives rather than mandates. One mandate—for newly constructed state buildings to meet or exceed standards for energy efficiency and indoor air quality—aligns with interview responses in the study that incorporating such measures at the time of building construction is less expensive than changing systems in an existing building and creates long-term cost savings.

This study suggests that passage of environmental and energy policies—and, by extension, environmental health policies generally—is more complex than a simple red state–blue state dynamic. While Hess, Mai, and Brown concede that some types of laws are unlikely to get off the ground in Republican-controlled states, they conclude that nevertheless there are opportunities to pass environmental (and related) laws that "can appeal to conservatives of both parties and to Republican-dominated state legislatures."

Similarly, a number of "red" states are increasingly budgeting funds toward projects to protect their coastal and other areas from climate change—although they may refer to "extreme weather events" rather than "climate change."[11] Framing and phrasing matter.

A major government effort to better connect environment and health via data collection and integration, and improve environmental health protection across states, is the CDC's National Environmental Public Health

Tracking Network. Established in 2002, it combines health data and environmental data from national, state, and local sources "and provides supporting information to make the data easier to understand."[12] States apply to the program in a competitive process. CDC funds recipients to develop and implement local tracking programs and data networks "to grow public health capacity and expertise in environmental health surveillance, and to modernize data systems."

The original intent was for the Tracking Network to be "a national program, national database, unified data resources," says Burke of Johns Hopkins. "Without that, states are flying blind."[13] Thirty-three recipients—thirty-two states and one county—are part of the network. (Note: This program was significantly cut in the first half of 2025.) One of the network's outcomes is a nationwide drought map created through the program's data exploration functions. Drought datasets include a drought monitor, drought severity index, and precipitation index. Another example is the Heat & Health Tracker, which connects data on maximum temperatures with data on emergency department visits for heat-related illness. The State of Florida uses the data from this tool to study the efficacy of kitchen faucet filters to reduce arsenic in drinking water from wells and for air quality alerts in schools to create healthier environments for asthmatic students.[14]

A 2017 assessment of the Tracking Network found that expanding the amount of community-level (such as census tract) data that is included is a key to ensuring its usefulness moving forward, along with the participation of all fifty states.[15] The authors also recommend building broader partnerships between the state tracking programs and academic entities in order to develop and test hypotheses via research studies, which should then be published. These goals align with the movement in environmental health toward looking beyond the risks of single pollutants to a broader examination of a community's exposure to multiple pollutants simultaneously, and incorporating the greater sensitivity of groups like children, pregnant women, and environmental justice populations.

PROGRESSIVE PROTOTYPES—AND INEQUITIES

The downside of the current regulatory patchwork at the state level is the health inequities created. Someone who lives in one of the dozen-and-a-half states that align with California's tailpipe emissions standards rather than the more relaxed federal standards probably enjoys health benefits from reduced air pollution—while residents of other states do not. That is also the case for residents of East Coast states within the Regional Greenhouse Gas Initiative (RGGI) partnership, which limits greenhouse gas emissions, and other hazardous air pollutants in the process.[16] A study that compared RGGI states with neighboring non-RGGI states concluded that "RGGI has provided substantial child health benefits," sparing children hundreds of asthma cases and reducing preterm births and cases of autism spectrum disorder and low birth weight. These health benefits translate into dollar savings, too—between $191 and $350 million.[17]

As a local example, Cuyahoga County, Ohio, adopted an innovative, multidisciplinary program to address housing conditions that worsened asthma in high-risk pediatric patients. It coordinated remediation for moisture problems, mold, and additional asthma triggers and provided weatherization for energy efficiency and other healthy housing improvements. Symptom days, emergency department visits, and hospitalizations declined significantly for the group receiving the intervention.[18] This was unique because improvements to indoor air quality—which is critical to good health, since it is where people spend most of their time and can be contaminated by a range of allergy and asthma triggers—typically address only one concern at a time, like lead paint.

Those who live in this Ohio county and benefited from this unusual, comprehensive program were lucky. Most people in need of this kind of service do not live in a state or municipality that provides it. While there is growing activity to connect housing availability and affordability with the built environment and health outcomes, such efforts are scattered and irregular; whether one benefits depends on coincidental decisions about where to live. An article about the Cuyahoga County program notes that key policy impediments to improving health in housing include "lack of clarity in statutory authority, and gaps in responsibility for the built and indoor environments."[19]

Perhaps no example of federal whiplash and scattered state efforts to fill the resulting gaps in protection approaches efforts to ban the insecticide chlorpyrifos. Chlorpyrifos is part of a class of insecticides called organophosphates that kill insects and other animals by interfering with nerve impulse transmission. Of thirty-six organophosphate insecticides registered for use in the United States, all can cause acute toxicity.[20] EPA banned chlorpyrifos for indoor use in 1996, but it is still widely used in agriculture and can be used on golf courses and to treat wood fences and utility poles. Health effects of human exposure can include low birth weight and neurological and developmental problems in children. A study by Dr. Leonardo Trasande, professor in New York University's medical, public service, and global public health schools, found that American children born in 2010 "lost 1.8 million IQ points and 7,500 children had their IQs shifted into the intellectual disability range as a result of prenatal organophosphate exposures."[21] At a high enough dosage, central nervous system effects of chlorpyrifos exposure can be severe, ranging from reduced motor function to breathing problems and paralysis.[22]

As table 2-2 illustrates, the federal back and forth in regulating chlorpyrifos has spanned about a decade. EPA planned to ban chlorpyrifos in agriculture, then reversed this plan; several states began instituting their own bans; a federal ban was back on, per a court decision; several more flip-flops took place. In 2023, a federal court overturned a ban; in response, in 2024 EPA proposed to disallow chlorpyrifos on food crops, excepting eleven com-

TABLE 2-2. A recent history of chlorpyrifos regulation

Year	Action
2016	EPA plans to ban chlorpyrifos in agriculture.
2017	EPA reverses this plan.
2018	Hawaii bans chlorpyrifos and requires evaluation of pesticide drift at three schools.
2018	Court reverses EPA and bans chlorpyrifos nationally.
2019	Appeals court tells EPA to make a decision. EPA: No ban. California bans chlorpyrifos. Other states do the same or consider it.
2021	EPA bans use of chlorpyrifos on food crops.
2023	Court overturns ban.
2024	EPA proposes to restrict chlorpyrifos, excepting 11 food crops.

mon ones, including apples, strawberries, and wheat. Hawaii, California, Oregon, Maryland, and New York have banned the use of chlorpyrifos.

For people who live or work in settings where chlorpyrifos might otherwise be used, the state bans, which still stand, can provide significant environmental health protection. Those in other states don't enjoy this safeguard—again, an inequity at the state level. Use of the insecticide has declined, however, particularly following California's ban. This trend again highlights California's influence, and it and the other states with a ban in place presumably provide a national benefit of reducing the overall amount of chlorpyrifos on the country's produce. Yet EPA's proposed continued use on numerous popular foods means that children will continue to ingest chlorpyrifos residue in their diets.

⁓

What is needed now to protect environmental health, says Burke of Johns Hopkins, is strength at the state and local levels. But instead, "it has gotten much, much worse because it is politicized and has lost funding." He points to the lack of state and local capacity to address urgent situations like high lead levels in drinking water in Flint, Michigan, the emission of volatile organic chemicals following the East Palestine, Ohio, train derailment, and increased flooding around the country: "We see a very fragmented approach."[23]

Given this challenging scenario, what can we learn from the experiences of states that have moved forward with their own environmental health policy efforts? Some general principles, which will be explored in the coming chapters, can be gleaned from the experiences of a number of states around the country.

- State-university-industry partnerships can lead to greater success than state governments acting alone when it comes to developing, implementing, and evaluating environmental health policies. Universities can play multiple, critical roles. They can carry out research and communicate it to state policymakers, thus ensuring that policies are based on the current scientific understanding of an issue and helping to ensure that the most important issues are prioritized for action. Academic experts can conduct cost-benefit analyses that provide clear evidence about the case for a policy—and where higher costs can be expected, like at the initial implementation stage, that information can help government agencies direct funding or other types of assistance to increase the support for a new policy and smooth its rollout. Public university extension programs are almost custom-made for this kind of role, given their mission to share "practical, research-based information" with communities.[24] Industry is also a critical partner, with its on-the-ground understanding of how industrial processes work and where and how changes can be made to improve environmental health outcomes. These kinds of partnerships are better positioned than a state agency alone to deliver hands-on technical assistance to make a change such as selecting and using an environmentally preferable disinfectant instead of a toxic conventional product in a school or other community setting. These principles are exemplified by the Massachusetts Toxics Use Reduction Act and the State of Texas's Integrated Pest Management law for schools.

- An understanding of basic principles of environmental and occupational health—how pollution is emitted, its impacts on health, the groups that are particularly vulnerable, and how to address pollution exposures—is foundational to the ability to develop and implement policies in this arena. Yet because medical students receive almost no education on this topic and there has been an erosion of environmental health content in master of public health programs, the resulting lack of knowledge can be a significant obstacle to progress in many states. In New York, the successful undertaking to build a state-funded, statewide network of both occupational health clinics and children's environmental health centers has gone a long way toward addressing this deficiency. By expanding training programs in these areas of environmental health and by emphasizing the importance of prevention in workplaces, schools, and recreational areas, the clinic networks have created a cadre of professionals who act as educators and advocates for environmental health policies.

- Community action and input can be invaluable in ensuring that local concerns and priorities reach state policymakers. This has particularly been the case for air pollution, given that EPA monitors aim to gauge the overall air quality of a broad area and can miss hot spots of air pollution emitted by a particular facility or industrial zone. Community action has also been central to efforts to address the greater exposure of

Black, Latino, and low-income communities to pollution, which are often very localized. These discrepancies in toxic exposure have their roots in historical practices like racist zoning policies that led to housing being built adjacent to factories in largely African American communities. Building on federal efforts, California has been a leader in analyzing how these groups can experience greater susceptibility to health impacts of pollution due to socioeconomic factors, existing disease, and other markers of vulnerability—called *cumulative impact analysis.* Via state laws like AB 617, the Community Air Protection Program, it has also carved out a central role for communities in identifying air pollution concerns and working collaboratively with state government officials to decide how to address them. Community groups demanded that their day-to-day experience of pollution exposure be taken into account in decision-making and problem-solving.

- A common obstacle to advancement of environmental health policies is the separation of government functions into separate silos. State public health staff often lack knowledge about the contribution of pollution and toxins to asthma—or the regulatory authority to address it. Public works staff, who select and apply chemicals like pesticides, typically do not have the background to connect these activities with health outcomes. Same for the sustainability office, which focuses on impacts to ecology. And so on. Recognizing the challenges posed by these silos, and that many policy decisions that significantly affect environmental health go by other names (housing, food, transportation, zoning, parks, purchasing, and more), some states are meshing agency functions that address environmental health using a Health in All Policies approach. So-called HiAP efforts are gaining steam around the country. The Tennessee Livability Collaborative, which has grown to include representatives of twenty-four state agencies, departments, and commissions, is a cross-sector success story. The effort has increased efficiency and reduced duplication, leading to expanded opportunities to protect public health. Colorado's HiAP program has its roots in a historical understanding of the impact of activities like mining on environmental health. At the same time, the state's HiAP efforts were largely bottom-up, that is, initiated by staff—specifically, staff of the Colorado Department of Public Health and Environment's Office of Health Equity. The goal of both improving public health and reducing health disparities has met success, with a range of innovative cross-sector activities and use of strategies like data sharing leading to significant cross-agency collaboration.

• Clean air in schools is essential for keeping children healthy and enabling them to learn. Yet this important aspect of environmental health has long been neglected, with many school buildings rife with mold, toxics, and inadequate fresh air intake and filtration. The COVID-19 pandemic provided a unique opportunity to right this wrong. Congress provided billions of dollars in emergency funding to address impacts of COVID-19 on schools. But the federal government did not provide sufficient guidance on how to spend it—leaving state and local decision-makers rudderless about the most efficient ways to use these funds. Investing in better air quality could not only have reduced the threat of COVID in schools, it could also have better prepared school buildings for the growing impacts of climate change, like hotter temperatures and increased air pollution. Decisions about personal protective equipment, indoor air quality, disinfectant use, and other issues that arose during COVID but started before then typically sit at the state and local levels. School district personnel are educators, however, and these issues are far from their areas of expertise. More than other policy areas discussed in this book, school indoor air quality is an issue on which it is appropriate for states to regulate. But the federal role must include a critical backbone of research, evaluation, and clear guidance. This scenario, of state responsibility but a need for federal guidance, is a growing one.

• Air pollution doesn't respect state lines. Water pollution crosses human-made boundaries. So do animals. So it makes sense for states to coordinate environmental health efforts in order to achieve greater efficiency and outcomes. Regional cooperation represents an in-between solution to the problem of gaps in environmental health protection. Cooperation across states is not a federal approach, nor a single-state solution. Neighboring states not only share a natural environment, they also tend to have similar priorities and cultures. The Regional Greenhouse Gas Initiative of Northeast and mid-Atlantic states and the Southeast Regional Partnership for Planning and Sustainability, bringing together Southeastern states and several federal agencies, provide two examples of a structure that, in today's era of bitterly divided politics, represents a hopeful, regionally focused approach to addressing environmental health challenges. As with some of the other principles outlined above, a goal is greater efficiency, achieved in this case by combining the knowledge and resources of a group of states. Especially given stressed state budgets, perhaps this cooperative approach is set to grow to additional parts of the country and to encompass additional environmental health issues.

Many of the best-practice state case studies incorporate some or all of these principles. While the overall state-level environmental health landscape remains fragmented and inadequate, characterized by peaks and valleys, a focus on these principles can help to knit together and further expand such protections across a larger number of states.

THREE

Partnerships and Technical Assistance

Reducing Toxics in Massachusetts and Texas

What if I hadn't had to start from square one in strategizing what to do about the broadcast spraying of pesticides on my neighborhood's lawns every spring and fall or the insecticide sprayings from trucks every summer? What if the state had taken a proactive approach to this issue? What if that approach had included developing pesticide-reduction policies, then girding those policies with information, conferences, hands-on technical assistance, case studies, and finally enforcement?

That upstream approach is often referred to as *pollution prevention*, or P2. It aligns with the precautionary principle, which prioritizes taking preventive action in the face of uncertainty. Even when there is considerable evidence that a chemical is harmful, like from animal or observational studies, there is typically some wiggle room for industry to manufacture doubt. After all, it is unethical to carry out an experiment in which we put a group of children in a room and spray them with a toxin, then compare the results with children in another room whom we don't spray. Many times, we have to go with the data we have. And even when we are confident about the toxicity of a chemical, reducing use of that chemical is often not a simple matter given concerns about the costs of changing current processes and the availability of safer alternatives.

Under the precautionary principle, the burden of proof is shifted to proponents of an activity—to the manufacturer of an herbicide to show it is safe, rather than to regulators to show it is harmful. It includes exploring safer alternatives, such as natural or organic options, and asking first: Is spraying actually necessary? The answer might vary, depending on the situation of a farmer confronting a devastating crop loss due to an insect incursion as opposed to a suburban retirement home seeking a golf course–style lawn and the quickest route to getting there.

A P2 or precautionary approach would have taken much of the burden off me to educate neighbors, request that they change practices and explain how to do so, and continually press the city on policy implementation even after a protective pesticide policy was finally inked. It likely would have resulted in less application of harmful pesticides in our neighborhood and fewer related adverse health impacts.

MASSACHUSETTS TOXICS USE REDUCTION ACT

That is the approach taken by Massachusetts's Toxics Use Reduction Act (TURA), adopted in 1989. The law applies to industrial facilities that manufacture, process, or otherwise use toxic chemicals that are included on a state list—either large amounts of such chemicals or smaller quantities of chemicals designated as higher hazard. These facilities must report their chemical use and carry out toxics use reduction (TUR) planning. TUR planning involves reviewing how and for what purpose a business uses toxic chemicals and identifying ways to switch to safer products or processes. While TUR planning is required by the law, implementation of TUR options identified by virtue of the planning process is voluntary. Covered facilities also pay a fee, which funds the implementing agencies to provide a wide range of services to users of toxics, including education, training, technical assistance, and grant programs.[1] The TURA list of Toxic or Hazardous Substances initially consisted of chemicals that were required to be reported by companies under two federal laws, the Toxics Release Inventory and the Comprehensive Environmental Response Compensation and Liability Act. Since then, the state has added or removed chemicals based on its own analysis.

While TURA is ultimately a regulatory program, a major thrust is equipping businesses with information and tools to enable them to reduce use of toxic chemicals and shift to safer alternatives. The state offers conferences, workshops, information, case studies, demonstration programs, grants, laboratory services, and a forty-hour course to train TUR planners to reduce toxics use in their facilities. These resources are available not only to regulated entities but to anyone in the state who wants to take advantage of them. The law and the programs that implement it emphasize identifying safer substitutes for toxic chemicals while also taking care to understand which potential substitutes are toxic and to regulate them too—in order to reduce so-called regrettable substitutions.

Three state entities play major roles in carrying out the law. The Toxics Use Reduction Institute (TURI) at the University of Massachusetts Lowell is a multidisciplinary research, education, and policy center that "sponsors and conducts research, organizes education and training programs and provides information and technical support to large and small businesses and community organizations."[2] Its outputs range from case studies of communities that manage their athletic fields organically, to a report on statewide release of carcinogens, to contributions to United Nations Environment Programme chemical control guides.

Second, the Office of Technical Assistance and Technology (OTA) is a nonregulatory agency that works with TURI to evaluate toxics use reduction as well as related benefits to industry like more efficient operations and reduced water and energy bills. TURA is designed to protect public health and the environment while also "enhancing the competitiveness of Massachusetts businesses"—and measuring benefits to industry is key.[3] OTA develops informational resources such as fact sheets and guidance documents on environmental compliance and hosts educational events. OTA's staff of experts visit facilities to assist with TUR and program compliance; when they do so, the businesses are assured confidentiality.

Finally, the state's Department of Environmental Protection oversees the law's reporting and planning mandates, licenses TUR planners, and analyzes the data submitted by companies to evaluate progress in reducing toxics use and waste, then releases this information to the public. The department is also charged with "promoting TUR as the preferred way to bring facilities into compliance with environmental regulations."[4]

The program is governed by an administrative council that decides which chemicals will be covered under the law. The council is chaired by the secretary of the Executive Office of Energy and Environmental Affairs and includes the heads of five state agencies: environmental protection, public health, labor and workforce development, public safety, and housing and economic development. Thus, issues are considered in a multidisciplinary fashion. There is also a stakeholder advisory committee and a science advisory board.

Initially, only large quantity users of toxic chemicals were covered by TURA. A 2006 revision of the law that enabled designation of chemicals as higher hazard or lower hazard brought smaller-quantity users of higher-hazard chemicals into the program. The council can designate ten chemicals per year as higher-hazard substances and up to ten as lower-hazard substances.

Origins

Examining TURA's origins, one wonders whether it resulted from a perfect storm of circumstances—yet clearly education, awareness, and partnerships were key. Following the 1979 revelation of chemical contamination of drinking water in the Massachusetts town of Woburn— the subject of the book and movie *A Civil Action*—investigations identified problems with additional drinking water supplies. At the same time, community members became aware of hazardous waste sites in the state and began to organize to oppose development of hazardous waste treatment facilities. This led to "the building of a statewide network of community activists," according to a history of TURA by Michael Ellenbecker, former TURI director, and Ken Geiser, emeritus professor of public health at the University of Massachusetts Lowell.[5] The coalition, which aimed to expand both worker and community right-to-know about environmental and occupational health risks, joined with academics.

Ellenbecker and Geiser point to the development of leadership and organizational capacity in the state, which created "a seasoned institutional structure that was capable of passing legislation," as a key to TURA's passage.[6] They also note that the advocates had a vision that people could be mobilized around health concerns in their communities to advocate to reduce or eliminate toxic chemical use in production, which would reduce or eliminate polluting facilities—the concept of toxics use reduction.

Additionally, Ellenbecker and Geiser emphasize the importance of advocates' "simultaneous concern for environmental and occupational health." While toxic exposures experienced by workers and by consumers and communities overlap in many ways, they are often thought about and addressed separately—an artificial dichotomy. Accounting for both together can strengthen advocacy efforts and ultimately protection.

Ellenbecker and Geiser also note that the bill was improved by a long development period that involved extensive negotiation between the business community and the advocates, leading to consensus. Money helped: At that time, the state agencies had healthy budgets and plentiful resources. And there was clarity: "Toxics use reduction, itself, was a strong concept with a clear message and a well-crafted definition."[7]

Outcomes

TURA's innovative approach has led to significant toxics use reduction. From 1990 to 2016, Massachusetts businesses subject to TURA requirements reduced their use of toxic chemicals by 66 percent. Additionally, they reduced toxic chemical by-products by 72 percent and on-site chemical releases (to air, land, surface, or groundwater at the factory or facility) by 92 percent.[8] Between 2007 and 2021, adjusting for an increase in production, the 2007 "core group" facilities (industry categories and chemicals subject to TURA reporting in 2007 and since then) reduced toxic chemical use by 62 percent. They also reduced toxic by-products by 41 percent, toxics shipped from the facility as part of products by 42 percent, on-site releases of toxics to the environment by 76 percent, and transfers of toxics off-site for additional waste management by 17 percent.[9]

Consider trichloroethylene (TCE), which the state added to the list in 2008. TCE is often used as a degreasing solvent and is found in several common household products, such as carpet cleaners and cleaning wipes. According to the National Cancer Institute, long-term exposure causes kidney cancer and possibly other cancers.[10] In a pilot project in Rhode Island to decrease TCE use, TURI's lab, in partnership with the EPA's New England office, held workshops and provided on-site assistance. This effort led to an 82 percent reduction in TCE use in two years.[11] A TURA analysis notes that in some cases, companies can eliminate the need to clean or degrease "by redesigning the production process" itself, in addition to considering safer alternatives. It attributes success in TCE reduction to both regulations and "the availability of extensive technical assistance."[12] So the combination of carrot and stick is critical, and under TURA, support to facilities to make healthier changes is comprehensive.

TCE also provides an example of the 2006 revision to TURA that added a higher-hazard category of chemicals. When TCE was added to the list with that designation, almost one-quarter of its use reported for that year was by facilities that became covered by the program as a result of the new, lower reporting threshold. Larger users had already reduced their use of TCE—for which there are a number of safer alternatives—due to both federal and Massachusetts regulations. This means of including additional facilities demonstrates how the program can expand in order to achieve greater environmental health benefits as program analysis identifies these areas for amplification. Further, a potential substitute for TCE that was mostly unregulated but is also harmful was listed under TURA in order to discourage its use and prevent regrettable substitution—and state staff carried out outreach to educate potential users of its risks as well.[13] Including lower-quantity uses of higher-hazard toxics such as TCE can reduce not only environmental health risks but occupational exposures as well.

A 2011 analysis of the program at its twenty-year mark that includes results of a survey of businesses paints a picture of how it creates benefits that go beyond toxics use reduction. Rachel I. Massey, then TURI policy program manager and senior associate director, found that the most frequent improvements of facilities complying with TURA were organizational, such as greater attention by managers to environmental practices, along with better worker health and safety and cost savings. Some of these sprang from managers' required consultation with employees as part of the TUR planning process. Working directly with these processes and products daily, employees came up with ideas that yielded a range of benefits—and this involvement also elevated worker morale. Some respondents noted that they already used management systems like Lean Six Sigma and that they integrated TUR planning into these existing processes.[14]

The analysis looked at which of the six techniques defined by TURA facilities were using. Most (63 percent) aimed to make changes via improved operations and maintenance. An example was installation of a temperature-controlled storage room that enabled raw materials to last longer. Others substituted hazardous chemicals with safer ones (46 percent); made toxics last longer through recycling or reuse, thus reducing the amount needed (46 percent); reformulated products (34 percent); and redesigned or modernized areas where production took place (28–29 percent).

Survey respondents also described challenges they faced. These included technical feasibility, costs, and concerns about product quality and customer requirements.[15] In some cases, for example, a product made with a less toxic chemical doesn't work as well. Customer requirements may be so specific that it is difficult to make changes. The technical barriers cited point to opportunities for assistance through research and technical support. Reformulating a product can necessitate communication with suppliers to identify a safer chemical and with customers to ensure that the end product will be acceptable. Institutional challenges included an emphasis on short-term costs over long-term cost savings or toxics use reduction.

Another critique of TURA is that while it requires TUR planning, as well as a financial analysis of TUR options, it does not require TUR implementation. However, this can also be viewed as a positive, in the sense that facility decision-makers maintain flexibility to choose options that work best for them. So when facilities do implement TUR options, they often aim to maximize financial as well as health and environmental benefits.[16]

Massey also describes survey results for community grantees, such as neighborhood dry-cleaning stores that were not covered by TURA but received small amounts of funding to reduce their use of toxic perchloroethylene. In addition to health and environmental benefits, they identified economic benefits, including marketing benefits for small businesses such as landscaping firms, and cost savings from reduced water pollution costs and fees. Respondents noted that the grant program gave them hands-on training to which they would not otherwise have had access, as well as assistance with media outreach and opportunities to develop new areas of expertise. Some successfully built on the TURI grant to secure additional financial support from other government sources.

Moving forward to 2017, an analysis of TURA carried out that year found that many businesses were saving on their annual operating costs "as a direct result of toxics use reduction or resource conservation efforts."[17] One case study looks at two businesses that applied TUR techniques to reduce their use of hexavalent chromium, a carcinogen, in decorative chrome plating. One made a large capital investment to modernize its system for using hexavalent chromium and nickel and install a closed-loop water treatment system that recirculates water for heating or cooling. These changes greatly reduced the use of the toxic chemicals, while also saving 147,000 gallons of water a day. The upgrades also increased the company's plating capacity and allowed it to remain competitive. As depicted in table 3-1, the company recouped its investments within about two and a half years, followed by annual (and growing) cost savings. The other company reduced its use of a number of toxic chemicals by making changes in its equipment, processes, and chemicals over time. These saved money, including by reducing the costs of managing hazardous substances. In shifting to a system that

TABLE 3-1. Savings and costs at two facilities offering decorative chrome plating

Facility	Project	Capital investments	Annual savings (costs)	Other business factors
Columbia Manufacturing	Facility upgrade; installation of new plating line; closed-loop water treatment system	$4,000,000 (approximate)	$1,046,000	New plating line tripled plating capacity; helped the company remain competitive and stay in business
	Energy efficiency		$500,000	
Independent Plating	Elimination of cyanide plating baths		Savings (amount not quantified)	Savings included elimination of cyanide destruction in wastewater treatment
	Hydrochloric acid reduction		$15,000	
	Elimination of organic solvents for cleaning		Savings (amount not quantified)	
	Substitution of ammonium bifluoride for liquid HF		$8,500	Improved occupational safety
	Addition of trivalent chromium plating line	$46,800 (partly offset by $15,000 TURI grant)	($20,204) (parentheses denote a cost increase)	Use of trivalent chromium chromium has allowed several customers to qualify their products for green certification and Leadership in Energy and Environmental Design (LEED) points

(*Source*: Toxics Use Reduction Institute and Office of Technical Assistance and Technology, "Toxics Use Reduction and Resource Conservation: Competitiveness Impacts for Massachusetts Businesses," TURI Report #2017-002, September 2017)

reduced use of hexavalent chromium, chemical purchasing costs rose—but the company saved on costs of managing toxic waste. A unique business benefit of the change was to enable several customers to meet criteria for green certifications for their products. The transition also improved health and safety in the factory and saved money overall. The financial outcomes are depicted in table 3-1.

Another motivation for companies to reduce toxics is complying with the European Union's typically stricter regulations. The 2017 report describes how one multinational company requested assistance from TURI to improve a diagnostic medical product that contains a chemical identified under the EU's Registration, Evaluation and Authorization of Chemicals (REACH) regulation as a "Substance of Very High Concern," which indicates likely future restrictions. Working with TURI to identify a safer substitute for that chemical helped the company prepare for future regulatory actions and thus increase the efficiency of its business operations.[18]

Groups brought together by TURI have helped create both toxics use reduction and efficiencies. The New England Lead-Free Electronics Consortium connected twenty-five companies to test materials that do not contain lead for use in a range of electronics items. The group was successful in testing lead-free alternatives and confirming that they worked as well as or better than those containing lead. The participating businesses noted the benefits of working together, including research that led to insights that enabled the changes and a faster schedule in putting the lead-free electronics on the market.[19]

Keys to Success

TURA's early start in P2 and its broad influence have inspired analysts to consider the factors that contribute to its success. Ellenbecker and Geiser point to the focus on facility planning, in which firms assess toxic chemical use and the availability of safer alternatives; the use of "independently trained and licensed planners," which extends technical outreach and information broadly; annual chemical use reporting that is posted online and "has made the program transparent and credible"; a steady, dependable revenue stream (in the annual fees paid by large quantity toxics users); input from the scientific community; and "opportunities for businesses to take a leadership role by integrating [TUR] into their core business model." Finally, the community grants program, geared to small local busi-

nesses, has enabled nail salons, auto shops, dry cleaners, and others to reduce use of toxics and spread their successes "to other businesses and communities."[20]

Michael P. Wilson of the University of California Berkeley and colleagues emphasize that TURA "requires firms to report their use of hazardous chemicals rather than their releases of chemical pollutants," the latter
being the approach taken by most environmental health laws. Additionally,
it is "the only statute that includes an institute [TURI] to provide ongoing
technical assistance, training, and research" to help businesses reduce toxics
use. "Together," they write, "these approaches have motivated continual innovation by firms in strategies to reduce their use of hazardous chemicals."[21]

Providing in-person technical assistance is central to the program's success. A study found that companies that received in-person visits from the
state's Office of Technical Assistance "reduced an average of 9.4% more toxics use after being visited than before." Companies visited by OTA achieved
far greater reductions in toxics use than those not visited, both in the year of
the visit and the year following.[22]

Dara O'Rourke of UC Berkeley's Department of Environmental Science, Policy and Management and Eungkyoon Lee of MIT's Department of
Urban Studies and Planning compare TURA with traditional command-and-control systems in which the government tells companies what
to do and how to do it. They see advantages to TURA's mandatory planning, combined with information resources provided by the state: "Forcing
firms to better understand their processes (and the costs of these processes)
and helping them identify options for pollution prevention through training, case studies of leading firms and publications, has led to an atmosphere
of innovation and learning in the state which helps even reluctant firms
change. . . . [F]irms realized that there were benefits to developing process
flow diagrams, conducting materials balances, identifying eco-efficiency
options and receiving training on developing cross-functional environmental
teams." Required planning, they believe, "has been able to motivate deeper,
more systematic changes that support continuous process improvements."[23]
This process differs from command-and-control regulation by motivating
companies themselves to make changes, in partnership with regulators.

O'Rourke and Lee make a thought-provoking observation, given that
much federal environmental health regulation is slowed as parties try to
come to agreement on the risk of a certain toxic chemical: Under TURA,
"uncertainty is acknowledged and accepted as a reality of problem solving.

TURA provides a more flexible process, ripe with dialogue and learning, that encourages technical innovation."

They observe that TURA is forward-looking in focusing on outcomes (by how many pounds a toxic chemical was reduced), not just actions taken; using market incentives to motivate firms to make changes; and ensuring that regulators possess technical knowledge and capabilities, just as the regulated firms do. (A recent national example proving this need are the calamities resulting from the apparent lack of technical understanding among government employees charged with overseeing Boeing's regulatory compliance.) O'Rourke and Lee emphasize as overall contributions to the law's success that the state provides comprehensive training and information, that TUR planner training offers education about the most state-of-the-art technologies, and that TURI's services are available at no cost to all interested firms, whether regulated or not. The history of TURA "shows that regulations need to transform the attitudes of managers, and then support their efforts at change. . . . TURA represents the potential for what could be termed a sort of 'command-and-innovate' regulation."

In terms of challenges, O'Rourke and Lee point out that while businesses participate regularly in TURA, it involves only limited public participation in its efforts. Yet they believe that public participation and public pressure are key to ensuring that firms not only plan to reduce toxics use but also implement those plans—which they may choose not to do because of cost concerns. They recommend that the state agencies expand public disclosure of TUR data—even compiling a list of "worst performers"—to increase public awareness of the program.[24]

Moving southwest from Massachusetts, Texas offers another example of a successful environmental health law that embodies pollution prevention principles, a strong state-university-industry partnership, and extensive, effective technical assistance.

TEXAS SCHOOL INTEGRATED PEST MANAGEMENT PROGRAM

As part of my efforts to protect my children from pesticide exposure at school, I asked the school board to adopt an Integrated Pest Management (IPM) policy. IPM is a well-established, common-sense approach that focuses on long-term prevention of pests. Nonchemical methods are used first—for example, sealing cracks in a building's foundation to block an entryway for pests or ensuring that a staff kitchen is kept free of crumbs that might attract bugs. Outdoors, practices that naturally strengthen the ability of grass to resist weeds are prioritized, such as setting the mowing height higher to enable strong root growth, along with fertilizing and aerating to reduce soil compaction and let air and water in. Chemicals are used only as a last resort—and when they are, the least toxic is selected and the smallest amount needed is used. Careful observation, recordkeeping, and communications with everyone in the community are foundational aspects of IPM.

Yet IPM is a term that tends to be thrown around without a clear understanding of its meaning. For example, regularly scheduled pesticide spraying is never a feature of IPM, although some who are unclear about the principles of this approach may say their regular spraying is IPM. It can be challenging to increase IPM adoption in the absence of comprehensive technical assistance since it can allow for some pesticide use and its parameters and methods need to conveyed in a clear and practical way.

As with other environmental health issues, the likelihood of success at the school district level is largely dependent on laws, policies, and supports—such as education and technical assistance—at the state level. Texas is a state that leads in this arena.

Origins

In 1991, Texas's legislature passed one of the first laws in the country requiring all public schools to implement IPM. The immediate catalyst for this expansive policy was a pesticide misapplication that caused a rural school district to close. At the same time, there was a realization that public schools were regularly spraying pesticides in school buildings, which was causing children to get sick—and was ineffective.

Texas has a sunset law, meaning that every state agency is regularly assessed in a bipartisan process. When the board that oversaw pest control in buildings came up for review, legislators reestablished it with IPM requirements—and it was signed into law by Governor Ann Richards. According to Janet Hurley, senior extension program specialist-IPM with Texas A&M AgriLife Extension Service, members of both parties "went forth saying, this is the best thing for our citizens."[25] A bipartisan, multidisciplinary approach that asks, "How do we best deal with this?" perhaps came naturally: Texas already had a large IPM program through the US Department of Agriculture's National Institute of Food and Agriculture and broad experience with a range of pest control issues. "Ag, urban, public health—you name it, we do it," says Hurley.

Under the law, every school must adopt an IPM policy and develop a written IPM plan.[26] Every district must appoint an IPM coordinator, who receives regular training. Extension was already collaborating with the state pest control board to train pest control professionals on safe practices in schools. With the law's passage, the university experts added a training series for school IPM coordinators.[27] The professors partnered widely in this effort, working with the state associations of school boards and school administrators.[28] Extension developed offerings, including a video series, regional trainings, direct assistance to schools, and quarterly newsletters. The partnership was built on a long history of strong state support for Extension and on Extension's close relationship with and provision of programming for Texas's 254 counties.

The law covers both buildings and grounds. Instead of developing a list of allowable and prohibited pesticides—seen as creating a burden in the need to maintain it—the committee categorized pesticides in green, yellow, and red groups. While there are no specific product restrictions, schools must justify their choices. They must do the needed research and implement IPM principles and practices, such as starting by cleaning the cafeteria or installing door sweeps to keep out crawling pests and rodents. Figure 3-1, "Approval for Yellow and Red List Products," notes that the use of yellow-category products requires the written approval of the certified pesticide applicator and use of red-category products requires written permission of both the applicator and the IPM coordinator. Required use of this form illustrates the great importance of proactive analysis, transparency, and recordkeeping in product selection as exemplified by the Texas program.

Success didn't happen immediately. A 2001 EPA grant funded a new Southwest Technical Resource Center for School IPM and enabled hiring Hurley to oversee the project. (Figure 3-2 shows Hurley in action.) This seed grant, followed by others, enabled the team to develop additional resources. One- and two-day trainings now take place across the state. Extension staff school visits include a walk around campus, using any pest problems for on-the-spot teaching.[29] Extension experts continue to train pest control professionals for licensing. And every school IPM coordinator is required to

---

APPROVAL FOR YELLOW AND RED LIST PRODUCTS

Description of pest problem:

_____
_____

Justification for use:

_____
_____

Application site or area:

_____
_____

Name of pesticide:

_____

EPA registration #:

_____

Green List products may be used at the discretion of the licensee.

Use of **Yellow List** products requires written approval from the certified applicator. A copy of the approval must be sent to the IPM Coordinator. **Yellow List** approvals shall have a duration of no longer than six (6) months or six (6) applications per site, whichever occurs first.

Use of **Red List** products requires written approval from the certified applicator and IPM Coordinator. A copy of the approval must be kept in a separate file in the pest control use records for the school and clearly marked as Red List approvals. **Red List** approvals shall have a duration of no longer than three (3) months or three (3) applications per site, whichever is first.

Approval of certified applicator: _____Date: _____
(**Yellow** and **Red List** Products)

Approval of IPM Coordinator: _____ Date: _____
(**Red List** Products)

Forwarded to: IPM Coordinator   __**Yellow** and **Red List** Products

Approvals shall be kept by the IPM Coordinator of the district for a minimum of two (2) years.

FIGURE 3-1. Approval for Yellow and Red List Products form. (*Source*: Texas A&M AgriLife Extension)

FIGURE 3-2. Texas A&M AgriLife Extension senior extension program specialist Janet Hurley and Wylie Independent School District IPM coordinator Tony Jacinto inspect a storage space of stacked chairs for pest issues at Wylie High School. (*Source*: Texas A&M AgriLife Research)

educate others in their district—teachers, staff, families, students—about their role in the IPM program, such as putting an item in an email newsletter that is sent to all school staff.

So everyone is learning and involved—which goes to the fundamental IPM principle that everyone has a role to play.

As noted, the Texas IPM program is funded largely through grants. Additionally, the program charges for required training workshops. School districts that host regional workshops can send staff at no charge. This allows those districts to send not just designated school IPM coordinators but also food service managers, administrative assistants, and grounds employees, so that a wide range of staff can benefit from these educational opportunities.

Outcomes

The program generates a range of benefits. In a 2006 survey of school IPM coordinators carried out by Extension, 75 percent said the requirements had resulted in more effective pest control; 53 percent indicated that the program had reduced the long-term cost of pest management, while 18 percent reported an increase in pest management costs.[30] In one case study, a large urban school district with forty campuses reduced chemical applications by 70 percent and used only environmentally friendly products, with no increase in the pest control budget.[31] While this report was written in 2006, Hurley says these numbers have been consistent over the past decade. Studies around the country point to benefits of IPM to children's health, including fewer allergy and asthma problems and increased attendance.

Keys to Success

The major levers of success, according to Hurley, are (1) a strong law, which includes fines; (2) the extensive education, training, and technical assistance that result from the broad partnership among the state legislature, state agencies, the state university Extension program, school districts, and the pest control industry; and (3) licensing.

Regarding the law's requirement that any pesticide use in a public school be recorded, Hurley says, "This is one of our biggest strengths." Transparency increases awareness, education, and improvement.

Inspection is the backbone of IPM and is required at several levels. Schools must carry out regular building inspections to look for pests and identify improvements to structures or landscapes needed to address any problems. Officials regularly inspect schools—and they also inspect commercial pest control businesses every three years, examining the businesses' records to ensure proper application of pesticides at schools. "It's a double verification," Hurley explains.

Several tools, including the IPM Cost Calculator,[32] can help connect inspection findings with needed improvements—and associated costs, which helps with budgeting and illuminating the link between investments and outcomes.

Ramifications of any deficiencies are clear. Noncompliance? Relevant school staff must immediately attend an in-person training. Does a school have an IPM coordinator appointed by the superintendent? If not, it must appoint one within thirty days. If a district does not complete every action needed to comply, a fine can be imposed.

Finally, licensing of pesticide applicators is a key to success. "If you are trained," says Hurley, "you understand the active ingredient, the label, the

Safety Data Sheet" that provide information about hazards and proper use. By contrast, custodial staff typically lack this level of knowledge. Extension further engages the pest control industry by giving continuing education credit talks on school IPM at regional and statewide pest control conferences. Under Texas law, only a licensed pesticide applicator can apply pesticides to schools. Such licensing sits within the state occupations code, "so the legislature pays more attention" and holds individual applicators to a higher standard, Hurley says.[33] In fact, the school IPM law itself is part of the state occupations code, further reflecting the importance of licensing.[34]

Information is continuously disseminated to school IPM coordinators. According to a history of the program, "As long as there are insects, vertebrates, weeds, and public health problems, there will always be a need for information."[35]

∽

The Massachusetts Toxics Use Reduction Act and Texas school IPM law share commonalities that explain why both are successful in protecting environmental health.

Both states start with a strong law that aims to protect public health and is crystal-clear about who is responsible for doing what. But adoption of a law or policy is only a start—it will only be effective if it is implemented and enforced. Both the Massachusetts and Texas laws make the written provisions a reality by establishing strong partnerships between state government, a state university program, and businesses to provide top-tier, comprehensive education, training, and technical assistance. Both TUR and IPM are complex. The involvement of the university programs lends the deep expertise, along with research and educational capabilities, essential to staying on top of the latest scientific and technical advances, analyzing the programs' effectiveness and costs/benefits, and providing education and training. Training and technical assistance are ongoing, as befits the challenging and continually changing nature of toxics use reduction and pest control.

Both laws include provisions for steady funding that do not rely on the ups and downs of state budgets. They include enforcement mechanisms and give agencies the power to impose fines.

In the broad toxics use reduction domain, TURA is widely viewed as a model. It has influenced safer-chemicals initiatives in states such as California and Connecticut and the Canadian province of Ontario.[36] Minnesota now requires the state health department to generate a list of chemicals of high concern as part of its Toxic Free Kids Act, and Maine requires reporting of chemicals in children's products as part of efforts to "encourage the use of safer alternatives and increase awareness of potential chemical exposures from common household products."[37]

The State of Washington, in a 2022 report, notes, "Unlike other projects, pollution prevention improvements may offer significant savings in often-overlooked expenses like regulatory compliance, waste disposal, and waste treatment." It lists these costs, such as discharge and permit fees for air and water emissions control, that can be reduced through pollution prevention.[38] This balance-type sheet could be useful for agencies or organizations considering undertaking TUR.

What could enable greater adoption of the TURA model? One article in the *Journal of Cleaner Production* notes the importance of a searchable database of chemicals that includes their identified health and environmental effects, as well as performance and cost criteria for making changes to toxic chemical use, to assist states in moving toward safer alternatives.[39] This kind of detailed information enables TURA staff to analyze and provide information about its impacts annually. It is also critical for policymakers and other experts to develop tools to increase adoption of safer chemicals and products, ranging from bans and restrictions to tax incentives.[40]

TURI and a coalition of states, government agencies, businesses, and other partners have worked together to develop such a database and other resources, which are available via the Interstate Chemicals Clearinghouse (IC2). The group shares data, assessment methods, and results for developing and promoting safer chemicals.[41] Their publicly available resources include a guide to developing safer chemical alternatives, a searchable database on hazardous chemicals/products and safer alternatives, and a compendium of state-level chemicals legislation.

The collaboration is based on the recognition that different states have varying regulatory systems and priorities, so "one size can't fit all," says Pamela Eliason of TURI. "The purpose of the IC2 is to look for ways that we can be learning from and building off each other's work." For example, several other states adapted TURI's project to help dry cleaners move from using perchloroethylene to wet cleaning. At regular meetings, states learn about others' efforts in order to apply them to their own priorities and needs. IC2 membership is open to all state, local, and tribal governments.

Its work has expanded to issue areas including PFAS, environmental justice, and procurement.

A potential obstacle to the goal of involving more states is that many states have pollution control, rather than chemicals management, policies. These focus on reducing toxic emissions to limit damage to health and the environment. But chemicals management aims to prevent or reduce toxic emissions from the start. So states that currently emphasize pollution control and would like to move toward the kind of upstream approach taken by TURA and IC2 will need to shift to policies that strengthen chemicals management.

Additional lessons learned about implementing these programs include the importance of state tracking of chemical use so that state-specific issues can be targeted.[42] An overview of voluntary approaches around the world (unlike TURA's primary approach, which is regulatory) notes that successful programs are characterized by sufficient, consistent funding and transparent sharing of program results—both central aspects of TURA's success.[43] By contrast, New Zealand's voluntary program is criticized for a lack of specificity, including the specific goal setting for pollution prevention that is a key aspect of TURA.[44]

When it comes to IPM in schools, there are many forums, model policies, resources, and implementation case studies available for those who want to learn about this approach. With the science and policy aspects of this issue clear and well-settled, making a change at a school or school district may be more a matter of education and advocacy. If there is not a policy at the state level, advocates should look to the municipal or school district level. It is difficult to implement IPM without a policy that enables broad, continuous communication and evaluation across time and across any changes in school or municipal staffing.

The IPM Institute, based in Madison, Wisconsin, is a national forum offering regular calls and many resources. Similarly, the EPA website has a model school IPM policy, along with voluminous resources.[45] Many states, in addition to Texas, offer resources and information. Alongside government information, the Xerces Society for Invertebrate Conservation offers detailed pesticide reduction information for farms, yards and gardens, roadsides, cities and towns, and natural areas.[46] Sometimes local organizations, such as master gardener groups, can provide technical assistance. If health and environmental benefits aren't enough to convince a city council or school board to develop a policy, the educational and economic benefits of IPM should be persuasive. Chapter 10, "Advocating for Environmental Health Policy," provides more detail about strategies to push forward effective policy.

FOUR

Environmental Health Education

Creating Training Centers in New York

Doctors are highly respected. So when the retirement home across the street from my children's elementary school would not stop spraying its expansive lawn twice a year with a high hazard 2,4-D herbicide that drifted to school property, it would have been helpful to have a few physicians to buttress my efforts to change these practices.

I received a letter of support from a physician with the regional Pediatric Environmental Health Specialty Unit (PEHSU). The ten PEHSUs around the country—funded by EPA and the federal Agency for Toxic Substances and Disease Registry—are a national network of experts in preventing and addressing children's health issues related to environmental exposures. But other local physicians declined my requests for support. The asthma and allergy practice I took my son to sprayed their own lawn—so the lack of awareness of this hazard extended from community members to facilities managers to local physicians.

Doctors receive little environmental health education during their training—typically just a few hours. The same is true for occupational health, which focuses on injuries and illnesses in the workplace. At the same time, there has been an erosion of environmental health content in Master of Public Health programs that train many people who take positions in state and local public health agencies.[1]

Despite the lack of training, all of these professionals must address the adverse health impacts of environmental exposures. And while there are differences between the fields, there are also overlaps and many opportunities to learn from each other. For instance, occupational health specialists may be the first to detect a health hazard because workers tend to have higher levels of exposure to toxics than community members in terms of length and concentration. When a factory uses a hazardous substance in producing a product, the factory workers will likely be most at risk, but if the facility vents the substance to the outside, the community could also be affected. A new occupational hazard can be the canary in the coal mine that triggers concern for both workers and communities. And workers may bring contaminants home on their hair, skin, and clothing, exposing their families. In short, toxics tend to cross boundaries, which is why it's important for health professionals to reach across silos and receive proper training.

OCCUPATIONAL HEALTH CLINIC NETWORK

Worker injury and illness protections remain inadequate, despite passage of the federal Occupational Safety and Health Act in 1970. The Occupational Safety and Health Administration (OSHA), part of the US Department of Labor, is considerably smaller than its environmental health equivalent, the EPA. Early on, OSHA saved lives through several key health standards. These included the 1978 standard that protects workers from inhaling cotton dust in textile factories, which can cause a respiratory disease called byssinosis, and the regulation protecting workers from airborne lead exposure. But the standard-setting process is extremely slow, averaging seven years or more for issuance of a new standard.[2] Congress may even intervene to slow or circumvent this process, as it did when OSHA quickly issued a standard addressing common and often disabling musculoskeletal disorders—Congress repealed it. OSHA lacks standards for common workplace chemicals, and many of its exposure limits were adopted in 1970, when they were already outdated.[3] While some states have their own OSHA programs with protections that go beyond federal OSHA, they do not make up for the many national gaps.

Origins

In the 1980s, concerned about the toll of workplace hazards, Dr. Philip Landrigan, a pediatrician and epidemiologist in New York City, worked with colleagues to sketch a brief proposal to establish an occupational health center at Mount Sinai Medical Center (now the Icahn School of Medicine at Mount Sinai). An existing clinic operated just one afternoon a week. Landrigan, new to town, saw potential to expand this resource in a large city with an energetic labor movement.

Funding for such a program would come from the Labor Committee of the Assembly of the New York State Legislature. Through contacts, Landrigan met Frank Barbaro, who was the assemblyman from Brooklyn, "a former longshoreman with a touch of asbestosis," and chair of the committee, Landrigan says. Barbaro, noting that there were medical schools located throughout the state, suggested a statewide study to scope out the problem, and provided funding to do so. "We brought together a big team—eighty or ninety people," Landrigan says. "We had representatives of all the main unions and representatives from medical schools across the state from Long Island to Buffalo."

The resulting study found that 5,000 to 7,000 deaths were caused in New York State by work-related illnesses annually, along with at least 35,000 new cases of occupational illness per year. These numbers were likely low, the authors noted, due to workers' fear of losing their jobs if they reported problems, the often-long latency period between workplace chemical exposure and disease development, and the lack of physician training about occupational contributors to illness and injury. The study also found that OSHA standards meant to protect against chemical exposure were often violated, and that of the 52,000 physicians in the state, only seventy-three were board-certified in occupational medicine.[4]

The annual cost of this burden, in 1985 dollars, was more than $600 million for cancer, chronic respiratory disease, pneumoconioses (lung diseases caused by workplace inhalation of dust or fibers), strokes and coronary heart disease, and fatal kidney disease.[5] Most of these costs were borne by the sick workers and their families because, lacking the opportunity to obtain an exam from an occupational medical professional, workers could not prove that their health issues were work-related and therefore qualify for workers' compensation. According to Landrigan, when the team submitted the report, the Labor Committee "loved the fact that we had the unions involved and that we had medical schools from across the state, so it was geographically broad."

The legislature provided funding to develop a network of six occupational health clinics around the state: the New York State Occupational

Health Clinic Network. The network's mission is to quantify the occupational disease burden in the state; improve prevention, diagnosis, treatment, and management of occupational disease; and expand training programs in occupational health. Its prevention-focused "public health approach" aligns with the New York State Prevention Agenda, which emphasizes the importance of healthy worksites, schools, and recreational settings and reduced exposure to toxic substances.[6] Occupational and environmental health are connected in the agenda as part of "Priority Area: Promote a Healthy and Safe Environment," as shown in table 4-1.

TABLE 4-1. Section of "Priority Areas, Focus Areas, and Goals," from "The New York State Prevention Agenda 2019-2024: An Overview," updated April 27, 2021. Accessed January 22, 2025.

Priority Area: Promote a Healthy and Safe Environment

Focus Area 1: Injuries, Violence and Occupational Health
   Goal 1.1: Reduce falls among vulnerable populations

   Goal 1.2: Reduce violence by targeting prevention programs particularly to highest risk populations

   Goal 1.3: Reduce occupational injuries and illness

   Goal 1.4: Reduce traffic related injuries for pedestrians and bicyclists

Focus Area 2: Outdoor Air Quality
   Goal 2.1: Reduce exposure to outdoor air pollutants

Focus Area 3: Built and Indoor Environments
   Goal 3.1: Improve design and maintenance of the built environment to promote healthy lifestyles, sustainability, and adaptation to climate change

   Goal 3.2: Promote healthy home and school environments

Focus Area 4: Water Quality
   Goal 4.1: Protect water sources and ensure drinking water quality

   Goal 4.2: Protect vulnerable waterbodies to reduce potential public health risks associated with exposure to recreational water

Focus Area 5: Food and Consumer Products
   Goal 5.1: Raise awareness of the potential presence of chemical contaminants and promote strategies to reduce exposure

   Goal 5.2: Improve food safety management

(*Source*: New York State Department of Health)

Why New York? The state was central to the Industrial Revolution in the Northeast starting in the early 1800s, alongside a history of activism to achieve workplace health protections, buoyed by a high level of labor union membership (three times the country as a whole).[7] It was the second state to establish a workers' compensation program.[8] Dr. Irving Selikoff, the father of environmental medicine, who was Dr. Landrigan's predecessor and mentor at Mount Sinai, worked with unions of asbestos insulators in New York and New Jersey to study lung cancer in these workers, proving asbestos to be a carcinogen.[9]

Outcomes

Each clinic employed doctors, nurses, and industrial hygienists. The legislature renewed the program every year and gradually increased funding. There are now ten clinics, along with a specialty clinic for agriculture workers. New York was the first, and is still the only, state with such a network. Occupational diagnostic and treatment services are available to all state residents, regardless of ability to pay. The clinics are funded from a tax on workers' compensation insurance premiums.[10] Each clinic focuses on regional needs and is advised by a local committee.

Reflecting the clinics' preventive aim, if staff see a patient from a worksite or industry with an issue that may reflect a broader hazard, they notify the employer and/or union and may screen additional employees. They provide health and safety education for some workplaces and industries and to other health care providers through clinical rotations, teaching in medical residency programs, and continuing education geared to primary care practitioners.[11] According to Dr. Michael Lax, retired medical director of the Occupational Health Clinical Center at Upstate Medical University in Syracuse, engaging with other groups involved in occupational health has led to preventive inroads such as developing recommendations to reduce ergonomic injuries that were incorporated by a number of employers.[12]

Staff have provided training on hazardous waste for operating engineers and health effects of pesticide exposure at a joint labor-management conference. Network presentations have addressed indoor environmental quality, green cleaning products, health hazards in hospitals, measuring toxics in the workplace, and strategies for safe schools, among many others. Figure 4-1 shows an example of training in the area of agricultural safety and health.

FIGURE 4-1. Jim Carrabba, New York Center for Agricultural Medicine and Health's senior agricultural safety educator, discusses safety when working near machinery with a power take off (PTO) and the importance of having proper PTO shields in place to prevent entanglement. (Credit, photo and caption: New York Center for Agricultural Medicine and Health)

The clinics had been in place for about a decade when the World Trade Center towers fell on September 11, 2001. Terrorists hijacked four airplanes and flew two directly into the towers. The buildings' collapse killed thousands and filled the air with toxic debris. Physicians from the clinic network, led by Dr. Steven Levin and Dr. Robin Herbert, quickly recognized the possible respiratory disorders that could result from the first responders' exposure to dust and smoke as they undertook rescue and recovery efforts. "Within a matter of days, we began to see workers who had been at Ground Zero," says Landrigan. The clinics treated them, studied their health problems, and established a program to screen the thousands of workers who experienced toxic exposures at the site.[13] The key, he says, was that trained medical experts were in place close to the site before the disaster and were therefore able to respond quickly. "By the time I left Sinai in 2018, we had 22,000 first responders in the World Trade Center program. This never would have happened—at least as quickly and efficiently as it did—if we hadn't had the clinical centers in place when 9/11 happened." Beyond occupational exposures, after the attacks many New York City residents returned to their apartments, making them susceptible to the toxic chemicals that remained both indoors and outdoors—accentuating the linkage between occupational and environmental exposures.

Recent clinic network data illustrate how work hazards have changed. Fewer of the patients who seek care currently work in industrial and construction jobs, while more come from firefighting, health care, and other public service sectors. A 2021 study describes the high percentage of patients seen at the clinic with musculoskeletal issues due to repetitive movements in their jobs and identifies "emergent" occupational hazards, including psychological stressors, substance abuse, and obesity. It pegs the cost of occupational disease in New York State at over $4 billion, with workers, their families, and taxpayers covering 70 percent of that amount.[14]

CHILDREN'S ENVIRONMENTAL HEALTH CENTERS

Children are also sometimes seen as canaries in a coal mine. Children are experiencing rising rates of illnesses that are strongly linked with hazardous environmental exposures. Asthma is a leading cause of emergency room visits, hospitalizations, and missed school days; air pollution, mold, and cigarette smoke can contribute to the development of asthma. As the diagnosis of developmental disorders like autism and attention deficit disorder has increased, lead, polychlorinated biphenyls (PCBs), and organophosphate pesticides have been identified as possible causes. Childhood leukemia has increased by more than 30 percent since 1975; benzene, other solvents, and pesticides are linked to childhood cancer.[15] Rates of preterm birth, brain cancer, dyslexia, and obesity have also risen in children. Figure 4-2, a graphic from the World Health Organization, depicts the sensitivity of children to the environment and the importance of protecting them from environmental exposures as early as pregnancy (and even before).

Federal actions addressing children's vulnerability launched with the 1993 publication of a National Academy of Sciences report on pesticides in infants' and children's diets, a watershed that led Congress to pass the Food Quality Protection Act (FQPA), which sets standards for pesticide residues in food specifically to protect children's health.[16] This new focus opened the

FIGURE 4-2. "Environmental Exposure Starts in the Womb," May 16, 2020. (*Source*: World Health Organization)

way for the creation of the EPA's Office of Children's Health Protection, along with clinics and research centers, including the PEHSUs.

Yet these resources remain inadequate. While the PEHSUs, typically led by physicians, carry out important functions in protecting children's environmental health—consulting with patients, reaching out to communities that have pollution that poses risks to children's health, providing information and education to health care providers and communities—they are limited by the responsibility of each center to serve numerous states and by insufficient funding. For example, the Region 5 PEHSU, based in Chicago, covers six large and populous Rust Belt states. And it does so with very minimal funding—about $150,000 per year. That amount has remained about the same since establishment of the PEHSUs in 1998. According to Dr. Susan Buchanan, director of the Region 5 PEHSU, known as the Great Lakes Center for Reproductive and Children's Environmental Health and based at the University of Illinois Chicago School of Public Health, these deficits severely limit what her group is able to accomplish. "You pick and choose," she says. "You usually focus where you're located, so most of our work is in Chicago. States go virtually untouched in terms of outreach, except for maybe responding to a question from a state health department once or twice a year."

Origins

These shortcomings were also experienced by the Region 2 PEHSU in New York. In order to increase efficiency, it was based at Mount Sinai and colocated with the occupational health center. "We took advantage of the industrial hygienists at the center and put a slice of their salaries toward enabling them to do lead and mold inspections in homes for the PEHSU," in addition to their workplace efforts, says Landrigan. "It dawned on us that we could replicate the occupational centers with a parallel network of children's environmental health centers."

Landrigan and colleagues followed the same process as for the occupational centers, this time working through the health and environment committees of the State Assembly. Again, they produced detailed documentation of the burden of disease and death from environmental exposures in New York State's children. They created maps to visualize the problem. "We laid it out county by county by county across the state," says Landrigan. "Every county has people in the state legislature, so we showed there was environmental disease in every county in the state and that it was killing kids and costing the state a lot of money."

They organized a broad coalition that included political leaders spanning both aisles, pediatricians and other health care providers, academic health centers, and environmental advocates. According to an article by Dr. Maida Galvez—a founding director of the centers that were ultimately established—and colleagues, many in the coalition had previously worked together on lead poisoning prevention programs and on the National Children's Study, a long-term national study of the impacts of the environment on children's health.[17] The group followed many of the same advocacy steps as the occupational health group. The state gave a small planning grant to the group to assist with development.

In 2017, after ten-plus years of advocacy, a five-year, $10 million contract from the New York State Department of Health established the statewide Centers of Excellence in Children's Environmental Health, more commonly referred to as the New York State Children's Environmental Health Centers (NYSCHECK). The centers are modeled on and have some personnel overlap with the PEHSUs, and they are also modeled on the occupational health clinics—but they are the first state-based model of its kind in the country (whereas the PEHSUs are a nationally based model). The Icahn School of Medicine at Mount Sinai functions as the coordinating center for the network and works closely with the seven regional centers, each of which is sited at a children's hospital. The regional centers cover every county in the state. "In this way," according to its website, "NYSCHECK serves as a national model for how statewide reach can be achieved. Together with partners, the Network has built a collaborative infrastructure across the state for EH [environmental health] education, screening, consultation, and referrals to needed interventions."[18]

Outcomes

Since its establishment in 2017, NYSCHECK has "served over 151,000 families, educated over 32,000 health care professionals and trained over 1700 future leaders, which includes trainees from high school to graduate school, residency, fellowship, and beyond."[19] The centers provide clinical consultations that emphasize environmental health screening to help families identify environmental triggers of health concerns, along with referral to local resources that can help to address such factors, such as home visiting to identify and reduce asthma triggers.

Centers use a tool called "Prescriptions for Prevention" to support clinicians in screening for environmental health concerns and identifying resources. These address more than forty different areas and are customized for the part of the state the patient lives in. Under "Cold Weather Safety," for example, prescriptions include space heater safety, tenant rights regarding home heat, and wood-burning smoke. Each prescription is about a page and a half long, written in a simple and straightforward style, and includes links to further resources.[20]

A major focus is educating health care professionals and trainees. To expand environmental health knowledge in state agencies, the program annually designates a class of "Environmental Health Scholars" who receive training and work on NYSCHECK projects. In 2023, two of the scholars worked to add climate and health education to their medical school's curriculum, resulting in the first approved environmental health concentration in a medical school in the state. Another initiative is "Educating Future Leaders Through the NYSCHECK Summer Academy," an eight-week training program in environmental health and advocacy for high school, college, graduate, and medical students directed by faculty from several of the regional centers along with partner organizations.[21] Regular videos and podcasts include the Sinai Environment and Health Lunchtime Chat Series and the Youth Symposium on Environmental & Climate Justice.

Center staff share information about environmental health with community members and lend support to policies and programs that will protect children's environmental health. For example, parents and local doctors were concerned about mold in a city's schools, so center experts provided information about how to manage mold exposure. In another case, an obstetrician contacted the center about a pregnant mother who had a young child with an elevated blood lead level. By looking more deeply into the issue, it was found that the mother restored old window frames and that this was likely the source of the child's high lead level. The centers shared information about steps to take to lessen lead exposures. In a child asthma case, a mother visited a nearby NYSCHECK center about her son's wheezing when he got home from school. Demonstrating the importance of considering the full range of possible environmental health exposures of someone with symptoms, a detailed medical history of the boy's possible exposures revealed that toward the end of the school day, diesel school buses were lined up and idling outside of his classroom. This seemed a likely culprit for his symptoms. Center staff informed the principal, who instituted a no-idling policy. This change greatly improved the boy's asthma.[22]

Keys to Success: Occupational Health Clinic Network and Children's Environmental Health Centers

What can other states learn from New York's experience? When it comes to the occupational clinic network, Lax echoes the importance of the network being statewide, not just New York City–based, noting that this heads off the "blue city in a red state" dynamic that often limits broad success and continuity when it comes to an environmental health policy or program. With clinics located around the state, says Lax, the network "has support all over the state." This principle applies equally to the children's centers.

Landrigan believes other states can make a strong argument for replicating the New York model of occupational clinics: "It is highly cost-effective. The cost of occupational disease is far greater than the cost of setting up a clinic." Savings include reduction of health care costs and the productivity losses that result when someone is taken out of the workforce. "The key elements are getting the partners to the table—especially labor unions—and working with them to co-create the program; doing a study to document problems in the state—all politics are local; bring in an economist; and have one or more champions in the state legislature and/or governor's office. And be patient—these things don't happen overnight."

The same goes for the children's centers: A 2008 statement of the need for the centers noted that their annual cost was less than 0.01 percent of the costs of disease of environmental origin in New York's children.[23] Lessons gleaned from the successful effort to establish the children's centers are recounted in a 2018 commentary in the *American Journal of Public Health* and summarized in greater detail in chapter 10. Briefly, key elements of success were building a broad coalition, meeting regularly with legislators, forging partnerships with champions in both houses of the state legislature, carrying out an assessment of the need for the centers that led to the publication of a formal report, analyzing the economic costs of pediatric illness linked with environmental exposures, mapping the presence of environmental hazards in each of the state's sixty-two counties, and surveying pediatricians (which revealed that nearly all of the state's pediatricians encounter illnesses that appear to be caused or worsened by environmental exposures but most lack information to address these conditions).

Galvez and colleagues emphasize the importance of state action during periods when the federal government pulls back from supporting environmental health. "During these times, state-based strategies provide an alternate pathway for advancing public health," they write, citing NYSCHECK as an example.[24] As federal regulatory protections and financial support become less reliable, this example of state environmental health protection stands as a success story and an example.

But how do we persuade state legislatures and other government bodies to provide more resources for children's environmental health? In a way, it seems circular: You need state funding to support environmental health education, but you need environmental health education to persuade states these programs are needed. The answer seems to be a combination of the various tacks the New York advocates took, although they started with a culture that was relatively friendly to their goals. In other states, advocacy may need to start smaller, perhaps aiming to get a small, initial development grant to start to make the case for such a clinic or center network.

Adding some environmental health education to medical school curricula may help to build a wave. Susan Buchanan of the Region 5 PEHSU notes the need for champions for environmental health education on medical school curricular committees. She points out that many environmental health issues have population-level effects; for instance, while studies suggest a link between exposure to flame-retardant chemicals and thyroid problems, it is hard to pinpoint that relationship in an individual patient, making it less of a priority for medical schools. Yet that leaves doctors prescribing thyroid medications while unaware of the factors contributing to the illness.

On a national scale, there are many risks to both workers and communities caused by the shortage of occupational and environmental medicine physicians and the lack of understanding of environmental and occupational health by physicians and others. For example, in a survey of first responders to the 2023 East Palestine, Ohio, train derailment, in which a train carrying hazardous materials derailed, only fifteen of 114 reported wearing a mask during the response. This was the case even though inhalation was the most common path to exposure from the toxic chemicals released from the disabled train.[25] Health care providers were not trained or prepared for this toxic exposure.[26] By contrast, in New York the existence of the clinic networks enabled 9/11 emergency responders and other workers to quickly access assistance.

Another recent environmental health concern was overuse of toxic quaternary ammonium disinfectants (or "quats") during the early months of the COVID-19 pandemic. While researching this issue after my younger son's school proposed to disinfect with a quat product throughout the school day, the most complete and clear information I found was on the website of the Mount Sinai Selikoff Centers for Occupational Health and Bellevue/NYU Occupational & Environmental Medicine Clinic. Use of quats is a risk for workers—and for everyone else, especially children. So the New York clinic network helped my own (non–New York) family and community through the information it made broadly available. Still, better occupational and environmental medicine training and education where I lived could have strengthened many of my local advocacy efforts.

The education provided by both the occupational health and children's environmental health clinics has a ripple effect as these professionals take their expertise into communities and hearing rooms. Landrigan notes that a key function of the New York occupational health centers, children's environmental health centers, and PEHSUs is to train the next generation of people working in the field—"and parallel with that, to be voices that speak truth to power in their state, their part of the country." With such centers established and funded, he says, "you have a cadre of people who can go and testify before city councils and state legislatures and argue for programs. It's incremental, but when you have the resources in place, it continues to happen year in and year out."

FIVE

Community Action

Improving Air Quality and Advancing Environmental Justice in California

Given children's sensitivities to toxic exposures, my son and his classmates should have benefited from special consideration by decisionmakers. But much existing policy doesn't make such distinctions, so a child often suffers the same hazardous exposures as an adult, even though their sensitive stage of development makes them more vulnerable to a range of short- and long-term health risks.

Low-income communities and Black and Latino communities, along with other communities of color, are also especially vulnerable to these exposures. While a child's vulnerability stems from biology, here the distinction relates to societal factors. Not only do these communities tend to be subjected to more pollution than their wealthier or white counterparts, but they are also more susceptible to its harms due to social determinants of health, such as less access to nutritious food and health care. For example, while air quality has improved overall in the United States since the enactment of the Clean Air Act in 1970, an analysis of air pollution emissions from that year through 2010, led by Yanelli Nunez of Columbia University's Mailman School of Public Health and PSE Healthy Energy, found that race/ethnicity and socioeconomics mattered in terms of who benefited from these improvements. In counties with a median family income greater than

$75,000, emissions declined more sharply than in poorer areas.[1] Similarly, Black Americans and those with lower educational levels are much more likely than other groups to live within a mile of a polluting facility.[2]

In some cases, policies themselves have created or contributed to the vulnerability of populations. For instance, the discriminatory practice of redlining, in which the federal government and mortgage lenders marked some urban and African American–populated neighborhoods as undesirable, made it difficult to get mortgages in those areas. Although officially banned in 1968, redlining contributed to a racial wealth gap that still exists—and wealth helps families to enjoy better environmental health. Redlining also meant that industrial facilities, and the pollution that goes with them, were concentrated in these "undesirable" neighborhoods, which further suffered from poorer quality infrastructure and services. Fewer parks and more highways mean more heat and toxics. Many of these inequities remain.

In response, the field of environmental justice (EJ) has developed to promote, in the words of the US Department of Health and Human Services, "the fair treatment and meaningful involvement of people regardless of race, color, national origin, or income in the development, implementation, and enforcement of environmental laws, regulations, and policies."[3] "Fair treatment" and "meaningful involvement" are the key phrases.

The official beginning of the EJ movement is considered 1982, although there were many efforts to stand up to such injustices before then. That was the year North Carolina's governor chose to dispose of thirty thousand gallons of toxic PCB waste, which had been illegally dumped along roads, by sending it to the town of Afton in Warren County. Of ninety-three sites considered for disposal of the waste, Afton had the highest percentage of African American residents.[4] Members of rural Afton, many of whom had been active in the civil rights movement, began planning a response. They registered Black residents to vote, protested daily against the landfill—which made national news—and opposed the plan to instead send the toxic materials to an existing dump in rural Alabama, not wanting to burden another vulnerable community. During this period, the US General Accounting Office (now the Government Accountability Office) found that in the Southeastern United States, three-quarters of landfills were located in Black communities and *all* landfills were located in poor communities.[5] To reflect these patterns of discrimination, activist Ben Chavis coined the term *environmental racism*.

Although the state buried the waste in Afton, African Americans were elected to local and state office following the widespread voter registration drive. The Black community vastly increased its political power and led successful efforts to pass environmental laws.[6] When the dump later required detoxification, the now-empowered residents insisted on, and were given, a seat at the table and a community-centered decision-making process. These efforts, along with a national study, "Toxic Wastes and Race in the United States," published by the Commission for Racial Justice of the United Church of Christ in 1987,[7] launched environmental justice research and policy activities around the country.

As national awareness of EJ increased, President Clinton in 1994 signed Executive Order 12898, directing federal agencies to address the disproportionate environmental and health impacts of their programs on minority and low-income populations. An analysis carried out some years later, published in 2019 by the Government Accountability Office, found that many agencies had created plans to address EJ issues. Yet most had not reported on their progress—or developed methods to gauge it.[8] So it was difficult to know if meaningful changes had in fact been made.

The 1994 directive was supplemented by two additional executive orders, both issued by President Biden: 2021's Executive Order 14008, which aimed to secure environmental justice in addressing climate change, and 2023's Executive Order 14096, which committed agencies to a "whole of government" approach to achieving environmental justice in areas including housing, energy, and transportation.

President Biden's Justice40 Initiative undergirded these actions. It represented a federal goal that 40 percent of the benefits of federal climate, clean energy, environmentally sustainable housing, and other investments would flow to disadvantaged communities "marginalized by underinvestment and overburdened by pollution."[9] This commitment was meant to direct funding under the Inflation Reduction Act of 2022—which promoted clean energy, among other goals—and the Bipartisan Infrastructure Law of 2021, which included measures to improve environmental health, such as ensuring drinking water quality. The Biden White House noted that a climate and economic justice mapping tool would help ensure the funds reached intended communities and that local residents were "meaningfully involved in determining program benefits."

Still, analysts have identified significant challenges that remain in achieving environmental justice. A recent article published in *BMC Public*

Health examines government failures to protect vulnerable communities from toxic exposures. It notes that Black Americans and other people of color and low-income community members are more likely than white people to be exposed to toxic chemicals at work, to live near industrial facilities and hazardous waste sites, and to use pesticides to combat chronic pest problems in dilapidated housing.[10] Children of color, who are more susceptible to pollution than adults and who face more exposure than white children, are "the most vulnerable of any vulnerable population subgroup," according to the group of authors, led by Nathan Donley of the Center for Biological Diversity and Robert D. Bullard of Texas Southern University (the latter well-known as the "Father of Environmental Justice").[11] They point the finger at government shortcomings, including failure to implement EJ executive orders regarding pesticides and protections for children under the Food Quality Protection Act.[12]

Additionally, although federal initiatives during the Biden administration included significant EJ goals, many researchers and advocates note that the playing field will never be leveled without action at the state and local levels. An article by several Brookings commentators, for instance, argues that federal laws like the Clean Air Act take a "one size fits all" approach that fails to achieve equity and justice—and notes, as context, that more people of color live in "fence-line communities" (close to polluting facilities) than thirty years ago.[13] This criticism is similar to that leveled at cap-and-trade programs—that they do not address unequal levels of pollution in different locations within the cap-and-trade area. The Brookings authors contend that the Inflation Reduction Act does not "legislate on justice" because it is demand-driven—reliant on tax breaks and subsidies that could end up mostly benefiting higher-income households—although they appreciate the planned use of a screening tool and funds designated specifically for EJ programs.

State and local government are key to addressing these shortcomings. To ensure the federal acts work as intended, states and localities can enact policies aligned with the federal efforts, help community partners in vulnerable areas access grants for climate resilience and other federal funds, and invest in community-based organizations.[14] Uma Outka of the Center for Progressive Reform—along with others—also emphasizes the importance of all three levels of government in protecting disadvantaged communities, noting the "significant role of states" in policy decisions, including permitting new industrial facilities.[15]

ORIGINS

The growing focus on environmental justice, paired with a better understanding of how vulnerable communities experience pollution, has led to the development of a new approach to studying exposures, referred to as cumulative impact assessment (CIA). California got an early start in developing this methodology when the state's EJ plan directed California EPA to develop guidance on cumulative impacts, which the agency defined as

> the exposures, public health or environmental effects from the combined emissions and discharges, in a geographic area, including environmental pollution from all sources, whether single or multi-media, routinely, accidentally, or otherwise released. Impacts will take into account sensitive populations and socio-economic factors, where applicable and to the extent data are available.[16]

The broad sweep of this definition reflects a sea change, from regulations that set limits for individual pollutants to ones that account for exposure to multiple pollutants from a range of sources. It also considers that age, preexisting health conditions, and genetics, as well as socioeconomic factors, can increase the risk of harm from pollution.[17] The goal is to develop a real-world understanding of how pollution affects health, rather than viewing each pollutant in isolation, as in a lab study or regulation of a single chemical. And California policymakers were interested in not just environmental health risks but actual *impacts*.[18]

California took its first steps in this direction following the US EPA's 2003 publication of "Framework for Cumulative Risk Assessment." For example, state scientists began to evaluate how early exposures to carcinogens affected cancer risk in infants and children.[19] Then, in 2010, California's Office of Environmental Health Hazard Assessment (OEHHA) created a screening methodology to evaluate the cumulative impacts of numerous sources of pollution in a given area.[20]

Obtaining this fuller picture of impacts starts by understanding a person's or community's vulnerability. A "relative ranking method" sorts communities by their levels of exposure to see which factors contribute most significantly to the overall pollution burden. This approach also directs resources to the most heavily impacted areas, identifying additional enforcement and incentive programs that could reduce the burden of pollution. Finally, it supports agencies that normally address one pollutant to work together on a range of pollutants in the air, water, and soil.[21] For example, perhaps a community located near a port is exposed to high levels of diesel exhaust, residents have a high rate of asthma and children have disproportionately elevated blood lead levels due to older housing stock, and the median household income is low. These would be considered cumulative impacts, and addressing them would fall within the purview of different agencies (health, environment, buildings, transportation/ports), which could handle these overlapping challenges more effectively by working together rather than in silos.

The framework evolved into the CalEnviroScreen tool. Version 4.0, released in 2021, is depicted in figure 5-1, which lists twenty-one indicators of pollution burden and susceptibility to pollution's health impacts. Percentiles, representing relative scores, are given to each geographic area. Under a scoring system, percentiles are averaged for the indicators in each of the four elements—exposures, environmental effects, sensitive populations, and socioeconomic factors—and combined via multiplication, as shown in the methodology illustrated in figure 5-2, to calculate an overall score that enables comparison of different census tracts.[22]

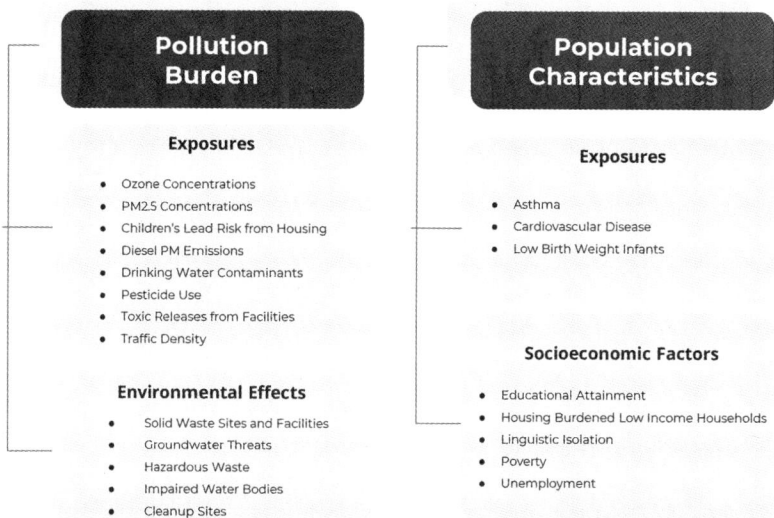

Pollution Burden

Exposures

- Ozone Concentrations
- PM2.5 Concentrations
- Children's Lead Risk from Housing
- Diesel PM Emissions
- Drinking Water Contaminants
- Pesticide Use
- Toxic Releases from Facilities
- Traffic Density

Environmental Effects

- Solid Waste Sites and Facilities
- Groundwater Threats
- Hazardous Waste
- Impaired Water Bodies
- Cleanup Sites

Population Characteristics

Exposures

- Asthma
- Cardiovascular Disease
- Low Birth Weight Infants

Socioeconomic Factors

- Educational Attainment
- Housing Burdened Low Income Households
- Linguistic Isolation
- Poverty
- Unemployment

FIGURE 5-1. CalEnviroScreen 4.0 indicators. (*Source*: State of California)

Pollution Burden		Population Characteristics		Pollution Burden
Average of Exposures and Environmental Effects	✕	Average of Sensitive Populations and Socioeconomic Factors		CalEnviroScreen Score

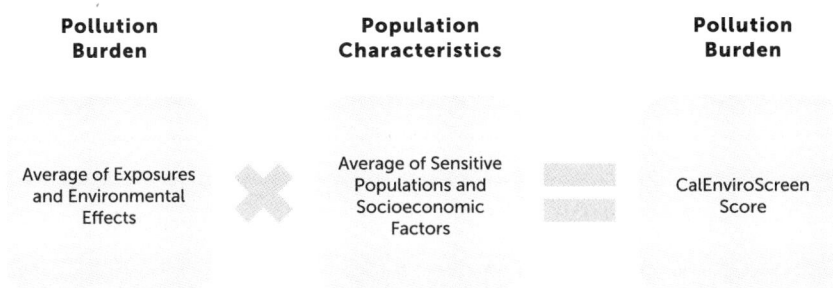

FIGURE 5-2. CalEnviroScreen scoring method. In the calculation, the environmental effects component is weighted one-half of the exposures component because the agency considers environmental effects to make a smaller contribution to pollution burden. (*Source*: State of California)

Policymakers chose to multiply rather than add factors because research has identified modifiers that affect risks of pollutant exposure. For example, numerous studies have found that asthmatics are up to seven times more sensitive to air pollution than those without asthma and that low socioeconomic status is linked with a three times greater risk of illness or death in a situation of exposure to particulate pollution. The maximum scores are 10 for pollution burden and 10 for population characteristics—thus 100 total.

As of this writing, the tool has been updated three times to incorporate the latest data and improvements. The 4.0 version, for example, improves methods for calculating some indicators by adding several pesticides to the pesticide use indicator, adding dairy and feedlot locations to the groundwater threats indicator, and expanding the hazardous waste indicator to include chrome-metal-plating facility locations. Analysis using the tool shows clear disparities, with Latino and Black people disproportionately living in highly impacted communities.

Air quality is a major focus of California's screening and environmental policymaking, and CalEnviroScreen is central to both of these activities. Air pollution has been a concern in the Golden State since at least the 1940s, when a particularly intense episode of smog—later determined to be caused by auto pollution—blanketed Los Angeles, with residents suffering from burning eyes and lungs.[23] The California Air Resources Board (CARB) was established to protect state residents from air pollution, which now also encompasses climate change. CARB consists of sixteen members, twelve of whom are appointed by the governor, and is supported by a staff of scientists, engineers, lawyers, and economists. The board carries out research and sets air pollution standards that aim to protect vulnerable groups. As part of the dynamic of iterative federalism, CARB's work affects national policy, and vice versa. Reflective of California's large size and economic and geographical diversity, CARB also partners with thirty-five local Air Districts, or ADs. Together, they provide grants and carry out regional planning, monitoring, and permitting of facilities.

While California has made strides in cleaning the air and has long led the country in its cutting-edge pollution policies, many EJ communities continue to experience high contaminant levels, especially near ports and inland from the coast. Informed by CalEnviroScreen data, in 2017 California's legislature passed AB 617, which establishes the Community Air Protection Program. AB 617 requires CARB to

- monitor "criteria" air pollutants such as ozone and particulate matter that must meet National Ambient Air Quality Standards, along with roughly 200 "air toxics" such as benzene, mercury, and perchloroethylene, which is emitted from some dry-cleaning facilities. CARB must also consider the need for and benefits of additional community monitoring systems, identify the highest priority locations for those systems, and deploy them in those locations;
- develop a statewide strategy to reduce air pollution in highly contaminated communities and update it every five years;
- select locations around the state for community emissions reduction programs (CERPs); and
- provide grants to community organizations for technical assistance and to support their participation in this effort.[24]

The law also expands the duties of the Air Districts, which must:

- increase monitoring in high-priority locations identified by CARB. They could also require a stationary source (such as a factory) that emits air pollution affecting that location to carry out real time, on-site monitoring, in which case the AD must provide data to the state;
- for those ADs that include a location selected for a reduction plan, adopt a CERP within a year; and

- in ADs that do not meet legal limits for an air pollutant, implement best available retrofit control technology for certain industrial sources on an accelerated basis.[25]

The law increases penalties for violations.

Community representation is central to AB 617, which requires that both CARB and ADs consult residents as part of planning and implementing programs. To ensure that happens, ADs must convene a community steering committee "using an open and transparent nomination process." Each committee must include community members who "live, work, or own businesses" in the area designated for local air monitoring or emissions reduction plans, although the majority must be residents. Members with business perspectives must also be included. Additional members may be participants or staff in local EJ or public health organizations, schools, local agencies, local health departments, universities, or labor organizations—with the final steering committee membership reflecting the diversity of the community.[26] Figure 5-3 depicts these and other aspects of community steering committees.

Community Steering Committee

FIGURE 5-3. Community Steering Committee graphic, from Community Air Protection Blueprint, 2018. (*Source*: State of California)

CARB provided grants to help community members participate in programs to reduce emissions, awarding funds for twenty-eight projects in the 2017–2019 budget cycles (at the start of the program). The agency then selected the initial communities to partner with the Air Districts to develop air monitoring and emissions reduction plans, involving residents and other stakeholders. This emphasis on residents' involvement in monitoring air quality reflects a growing push for community-based participatory research, a model in which local organizations and individuals work with researchers as equal partners. The underlying idea is that community members, based on their day-to-day experiences, bring significant insights and information to developing research questions and methods and analyzing data. In the context of AB 617, it is important to ensure that environmental health monitoring benefits the community itself; this is not an academic exercise but a program intended to make tangible improvements in people's health.

Interestingly, the initial purpose of AB 617 was to continue the state's cap-and-trade program, which was designed to reduce greenhouse gas emissions. But for all of its potential benefits, cap-and-trade can enable polluting facilities, which are often located in EJ communities, to keep polluting as long as they buy credits. State legislators from the powerful Latino caucus demanded that if cap-and-trade was to continue, the law needed to address community environmental concerns. They prevailed, and those components were included.

CARB published a blueprint to guide implementation. In 2018, ten communities with poor air quality, largely measured by their CalEnviro-Screen ranking, were chosen to work with Air Districts as part of the program. That number has since about doubled.

OUTCOMES

Frustration arose in the initial years of the law's implementation. The California Environmental Justice Alliance (CEJA) was concerned that concrete measures to reduce air pollution were limited. Yes, polluters were required to more quickly adopt retrofit technology and faced increased penalties for violations. But where were the results? Communities, they stated in a report, need "quantifiable, permanent, and enforceable" emissions reductions.[27] (A 2022 revision to AB 617 addressed some of these concerns, as described below.)

CEJA also had doubts about the process. For instance, did some members of the steering committees have conflicts of interest? Was it appropriate to include members who represented polluting industries, or even residents employed by those industries? Another issue was that some materials were left untranslated, which led some non-English speakers to stop participating. Perhaps most important, limited resources meant that many locations had to compete for just ten spots as "AB 617 communities."[28]

To spread the benefits of AB 617, CEJA recommended focusing on the polluting activities themselves rather than singling out a few vulnerable communities for protection. In the organization's vision, communities would advise the state on how to prioritize polluting activities or sectors, such as stationary sources like refineries or auto body shops, and broad sources like pesticides used in agriculture. The state or relevant Air District would then set targets and develop regulations to reduce emissions.

CEJA believes this approach would be more effective at reducing harmful emissions across the state and transitioning polluting industries that are now largely based in EJ communities to safer practices. The goal is better health for both workers and communities, along with simplifying enforcement due to uniform regulations across various areas. It would require policymakers to identify safer and greener practices in some industries and potentially to mandate emissions control for polluting industries on a statewide basis.[29]

Another major challenge of AB 617 is that it governs only CARB and the Air Districts, not other state agencies or local governments. Local governments maintain authority over land use decisions, which have a major impact on air pollution. While the locally based Air Districts have authority to control emissions from stationary sources like factories and power plants, EJ communities often live near shipyards and highways—and reducing those exposures requires changes in land use, such as prohibiting polluting industries from operating near residential areas or schools. That power rests with city planning and zoning departments. According to Jonathan London, professor of community and regional development at the University of California Davis and the principal author of a report evaluating community engagement under AB 617, it is a "major contradiction" that the bill is implemented through CARB and Air Districts, which lack land use authority.

This significant problem has been partially offset by another important California law: AB 1000, which requires local governments to identify disadvantaged communities within their jurisdictions and address EJ in their plans. In fact, California municipalities have developed an array of creative policies. For example, National City's amortization ordinance aims to cut down on polluting activities that do not meet new zoning codes. Typically, governments grandfather in existing land uses so that businesses can continue to operate even when they no longer comply with the new zoning. This meant that in National City, a largely Latino area where homes were often located next to auto body shops and chemical supply businesses, residents were exposed to high levels of pollution. The planning commission ranked these activities in terms of their harm to the community and started to phase them out once the owners had recouped their costs. Auto body shops were moved to a more sustainable Green Industrial Auto Park away from residential locations.[30] Similarly, Los Angeles developed a "green zone" designation for highly polluted neighborhoods, prioritizing them for additional city inspections and enforcement, more citizen participation, and "more health-protective standards" for new and expanded businesses.[31]

Regardless of this progress, experts believe more can be done to advance environmental justice by improving implementation of AB 617. Jonathan London and his colleagues at UC Davis made a raft of recommendations in their report, particularly when it comes to reducing emissions, the "clear central goal" of the law.[32] These changes include the following:

- identifying community priorities, such as renewable energy subsidies and diesel truck rerouting, at the start of the process, as opposed to Air Districts suggesting possible actions and then requesting the community's feedback. Solutions would still be informed by technical advice from the AD.[33]
- measuring the success of pollution reduction plans through health metrics as well as emissions reductions, as some steering committee members advocate. The authors acknowledge that it can be difficult to draw a straight line between reducing emissions and better health, such as fewer hospital visits, and that this kind of analysis would require closer partnerships with health agencies and researchers.[34]

Following several years of AB 617 implementation, the legislature passed AB 1749 in 2022.[35] It requires better reporting, calling for CARB to identify actions to reduce pollution in each state strategy update and for Air Districts to report on how their CERP programs cohere with updates to the statewide strategy. The goal is to improve accountability for actual emissions reductions by better integrating CERPs with other aspects of air quality regulation.

An updated blueprint, known as 2.0, was issued in 2023. It was informed by the previous five years of experience and by the "People's Blueprint" that was developed by EJ leaders with CARB support. It outlines a number of goals, including continuing to reduce pollution beyond the initial five-year implementation period, measuring and reporting CERP progress, supporting the more than sixty communities nominated to participate but not selected, and taking regulatory action to further reduce pollution. CARB will address mobile pollution (trucks, trains, etc.) both statewide and at the community level and support Air Districts as they implement AB 617 requirements for stationary sources (factories, industrial operations).[36]

Through "Community Air Grants," Blueprint 2.0 helps the government and community steering committees co-create CERPs. While this was envisioned in the original plan, some communities did not feel fully included in the process. The grants support communities in developing local CERPs in partnership with CARB and ADs, to ensure that the community provides direction to the agencies. Figure 5-4, from Blueprint 2.0, depicts these new emphases.

The final goal is to make air quality information more accessible to communities. This includes information about stationary source permitting, educational videos, and a reporting system to culminate in an annual air pollution report. In response to community complaints of shortcomings in enforcement, the document highlights how government agencies are prioritizing investigations and enforcement in areas identified by the community. For example, CARB worked with the state's oil and natural gas oversight agency to emphasize inspections of oil and gas wells in communities concerned about them. The state is expanding incentives for cleaner technology and practices to speed up emissions reductions in areas of community concern.[37]

Blueprint 2.0 addresses the state-local question in great detail.[38] It explains that cities and counties are in charge of land use, planning, zoning, allowed uses of land, and mitigation measures such as creating a buffer between agricultural areas and schools. As an example of state and local agencies working together, the San Joaquin Valley Air Pollution Control District and Arvin/Lamont Community Steering Committees partnered with Kern County and the City of Arvin to fund road pavement projects, add sidewalks, and make intersections healthier by reducing dust and other road ex-

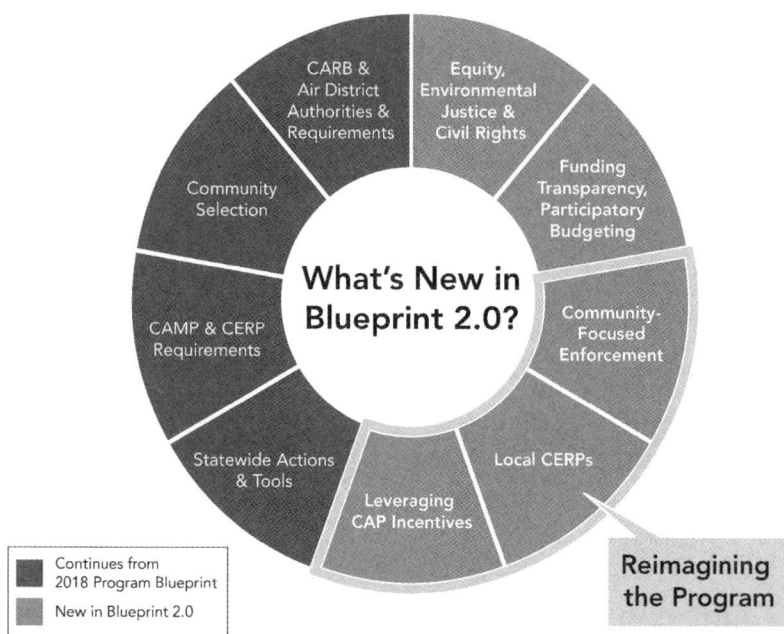

FIGURE 5-4. "What's New in Blueprint 2.0?," from Community Air Protection Program Blueprint 2.0 (*Source*: State of California)

posures. And the San Joaquin Valley Air District worked with all four community steering committees in its ambit, as well as local transportation agencies, to reroute diesel trucks away from residential areas.[39] As the Blueprint notes, it is "crucial to establish these partnerships with land use agencies early in the process" to ensure that community concerns are addressed.

London also believes the state should better integrate these roles to allow AB 617 to address land use. He gives the example of a city considering siting a warehouse in a community that participates in the state program: How do decision-makers overlay local and 617 policies in their deliberations? Air Districts could develop more collaborative relationships with cities and counties and become more engaged in land use planning. That could help them better coordinate clean air plans and implementation tools. Legal or policy solutions, incentives, education, and grant money could all help. London says 617 funds for cities and counties "could enable them to come to the table more fully." He recommends that the legislature revisit 617 authorization language to include additional state agencies "so that there is a larger mandate." This comment points to a Health in All Policies approach in which a range of agencies whose actions affect air quality work together. For example, some pesticides are designated as toxic air contaminants, but they are primarily regulated by the state's pesticide agency, with CARB having limited authority. Bringing the pesticide agency to the table could provide further protection.

The learning process has garnered results. "The agency staff really had to come to terms with environmental justice," says Dr. John Balmes, an environmental health professor at the University of California Berkeley and physician member of CARB since 2008. "They had to learn a lot—to go from classic air quality management and climate change mitigation at the state level to learning how to engage with communities. And that's where it's been really, truly transformative." There is now an EJ committee that advises on CARB policies. AB 617 steering committee members are compensated for their effort and are helping to decide how funds should be used.

Beyond AB 617, CalEnviroScreen is employed in numerous state programs. The Department of Toxic Substances Control uses it to prioritize inspections, investigations, and enforcement actions and to permit hazardous waste facilities. The Department of Pesticide Regulation uses it in making monitoring decisions and in selecting projects in which parties must take steps to reduce public health harm due to enforcement actions.[40]

London also notes the progression from an emission reduction focus to exposure reduction. Some actions being included in plans "are public health measures—vegetation barriers, electric vehicles and lawnmowers," he says. "People said, 'Yes, you would get X tons of PM [particulate matter] reduction from this locomotive [as an example of an emission reduction]. But we don't live near the locomotive—that doesn't really help us.'" London credits CARB for being open to approving CERPs that include such measures. Blueprint 2.0 notes that "health protective exposure mitigation measures and practices, like indoor air filtration and urban greening" can help reduce exposures close to emissions sources. And AB 617 and related programs can act as a catalyst for a range of local agencies to work with public health agencies to consider public health goals in decisions that affect air quality.[41]

KEYS TO SUCCESS

AB 617 was groundbreaking and trendsetting. The UC Davis report, although it made numerous suggestions for strengthening the program, described AB 617 as "a bold new approach to cleaning the air in disadvantaged communities through unprecedented public participation, local air monitoring, and comprehensive plans for achieving air emissions reductions in order to reduce health disparities."[42] Balmes agrees that the law's focus on community involvement is "particularly innovative." He points to the community steering committees empowered to work with local Air Districts and the grant money to help communities "work with experts and be closer to equal footing with their ADs."

Balmes also identifies local monitoring to identify air pollution hot spots as an innovation. This type of monitoring does not routinely take place, because EPA sensors are spread out geographically and may not capture differences in air quality between specific areas. In fact, they are meant to capture the air quality of a relatively large area, so placing a monitor close to a major air pollution emitter would hinder that goal. By contrast, community monitoring is designed to pinpoint specific areas of concern.

California has more than 250 air monitoring stations that measure compliance with federal, state, and local regulations. For AB 617 purposes, Blueprint 2.0 lists fourteen elements to take into account in developing an air monitoring plan. CARB provides descriptions of measurement technologies, along with their availability and cost. For four groups of pollutants—particulate matter, volatile organic compounds, toxic metals, and gaseous criteria air pollutants like ozone and nitrogen oxides—the agency outlines technologies that can be used to meet certain goals. One goal is to identify sources of pollution in a community; this can require different kinds of data and technology. Another is to inform public health research through air monitoring that quantifies the public's exposure to pollutants. This includes personal exposure research using technology such as small, portable air sensors that a person can carry around over the course of the day. Identifying pollution hot spots where a certain pollutant is concentrated, typically located close to an emission source and sometimes for just a short period of time, may require technologies "ranging from mobile monitoring, satellite remote sensing, dense networks of air sensors, or fixed monitoring sites."[43]

For example, San Joaquin Valley communities selected for AB 617 use a range of air monitoring platforms, such as "high-precision" equipment on trailers, vans, portable systems that measure multiple pollutants, and others that analyze single pollutants. These choices are meant to achieve an air monitoring approach that is "portable, scalable, and able to be rapidly deployed."[44]

Under AB 617, Air Districts work with their community steering committee to decide where to place monitors, whether by a school or near a factory. Program funds cover the cost of purchasing and maintaining monitoring equipment. Once the data is collected from the monitors and hot spots are identified, a CERP is developed to reduce those hot spots using the best available control technology.

According to the UC Davis evaluation, community air monitoring programs are innovative because of both their local focus and community engagement in deciding what pollutants to monitor and how. "This appeared to be an excellent example of science communication and translation," the report notes, and at least one community successfully made use of low-cost sensors, buttressed by Air District support to ensure data quality and education about using them. Several additional communities also used information gleaned from local air monitoring. However, this was more the case for participating communities with existing EJ organizations and experience, which were better prepared to realize these accomplishments. The UC Davis report therefore emphasizes that when CARB selects communities with less capacity, it should provide additional support.[45] One example of a community that already had a strong foundation in EJ work is West Oakland, cited as a model for advanced monitoring efforts.

According to the 2021 report on CalEnviroScreen 4.0, states including Washington, New York, and Michigan have used California's screening tool to inform development of their own tools specific to their EJ challenges. And the US EPA has "studied [CalEnviroScreen] in developing its own national screening tool, EJSCREEN."

What steps can other states take to follow California's lead? Charles Lee, author of an early EJ report, advises, "Start with mapping"—making use of replicable models like CalEnviroScreen's methodology and EJSCREEN's data (which contains national data), combined with state or local data.[46] (EJSCREEN was removed from the EPA website in early 2025 but may be available elsewhere.) By using data and mapping tools, states can layer pollution data and demographic data to better understand cumulative impacts. This information enables them to more effectively invest resources to promote health in these overburdened communities. Lee emphasizes the importance of partnership among communities, academic experts, and government in designing EJ mapping tools and of "experiential knowledge" from outside of government in applying these tools. He notes that viability of these tools depends on government bodies both endorsing and using them.[47]

For other states that want to protect vulnerable groups from air pollution, Balmes recommends joining the seventeen states and the District of Columbia that follow California's more-stringent-than-federal vehicle emissions standards. He also recommends they commit to a policy of using only renewable energy. And a state's environmental agency should go beyond meeting the limits for criteria air pollutants to address the hot spots of air pollution that disproportionately impact low-income communities of color. "That's totally doable," he says, given the availability of low-cost sensors like PurpleAir that can measure fine particulates. Those measurements help locate pollution and identify polluters that regulators may not know about. When states have that information, they can design policies to address those exposures. And increased monitoring can lead to stronger enforcement action, which CARB is carrying out as required by AB 617.

London says other states can learn from California's improvements in community partnerships with Air Districts via frequent (typically monthly) meetings and professional facilitators who are "flexible and skillful" at managing the meetings and their inevitable conflicts. "Invest in process. Invest in people who know what they're doing," he says. "States could ask at the start, 'What does it look like to have communities in the driver's seat?'"

Further, states can study CARB's blueprints that provide a roadmap for implementing this work—especially 2.0, which includes examples of activities, lessons learned from AB 617 implementation, and clear explanations of both mandates and optional activities for government agencies. All of these can easily apply to other states.

Finally, states can learn from California's experience by involving both additional agencies that influence air quality and municipalities from the outset. These partnerships could include carrying out health impact assessments, which would inform emission reduction plans and help regulators and communities prioritize actions. While the specific steps to improve air quality will vary by place, the common goal is harnessing community knowledge to protect vulnerable residents—and ultimately to achieve environmental justice.

SIX

Collaboration Across Agencies

Health in All Policies in Tennessee and Colorado

When I discovered that pesticide use by neighbors, along with nearby industrial and vehicle pollution, may have caused or at least contributed to my son's asthma, I looked to the city and state for help in reducing those triggers. I found that, at the city level, health department staff were largely unaware that pollution and toxics could cause or worsen asthma. Meanwhile, public works staff, who applied pesticides and purchased vehicles and equipment, did not connect these activities with health outcomes. The same was true for the sustainability office, which focused on impacts to ecology. And so on. State agencies seemed to be even more siloed, not to mention seemingly distant and remarkably slow to respond.

I was at the center of a pinwheel: The various departments spun around, but when I reached out, I could only touch one at a time. As they circled, they never connected with each other, each in their own separate realm.

Many policy decisions that significantly affect health are not labeled "health." These include actions around housing, food, transportation, zoning, parks, and purchasing of everything from school buses to cleaning products. Evidence suggests that involving experts and agencies beyond those focused on health in government decision-making can improve health outcomes. But from an organizational perspective, what could lead a transportation department official to become involved in asthma programs, when this may go beyond their job description and their statutory mandate?

What requirements or incentives would need to be in place for that to happen? What would it take for people from different agencies to work together given that government staff often not only lack incentives to do so but may have disincentives?

Working across agencies to protect health is often referred to as Health in All Policies (HiAP). According to the National Association of County & City Health Officials (NACCHO), HiAP emphasizes breaking down silos to achieve common health goals.[1] NACCHO's strategies for implementing HiAP include the following:

- Develop cross-sector relationships, ranging from councils and task forces to short-term workgroups.
- Use a range of tools to incorporate health into decision-making, such as health impact assessments and community health assessments.
- Expand workforce capacity by giving staff opportunities to work across agencies and by hiring nontraditional staff, including city planners for health agencies (and vice versa).
- Harmonize funding and investments, working across agencies and with partners to incorporate health considerations into funding applications and awards.
- Connect research, evaluation, and data systems to measure the impact of cross-cutting initiatives on health outcomes.
- Coordinate communications, such as a range of agencies raising awareness about climate change and health.
- Develop accountability structures, such as public reporting and performance measures on HiAP initiatives.[2]

In 2018, the Association of State and Territorial Health Officials (ASTHO) identified four phases of HiAP implementation:

- Informational: Partners build relationships and exchange information to increase awareness of the links between public health and other sectors.
- Consultative: The lead agency provides input and advice to other partners.
- Engaging: Consulting partners work more closely with the lead agency and may participate in policy implementation.

- Collaborative: Communities identify where they fall within a spectrum of HiAP activities.

These phases reflect a spectrum, and ASTHO notes that they may happen in various orders and overlap.[3]

Fortunately, HiAP efforts are growing around the country. Two states often seen as successful in this arena are Tennessee and Colorado.

TENNESSEE LIVABILITY COLLABORATIVE

States and cities that have undertaken efforts to increase agency collaboration call them different names—sometimes aiming to be politically neutral—and organize them in a range of ways. Some use the term Health in All Policies; some contain elements of HiAP but do not use the phrase. "The language and nomenclature have to be adapted to each location," says Sandra Whitehead, associate professor and program director of the Sustainable Urban Planning Program at George Washington University and president of the Society of Practitioners of Health Impact Assessment (also known as the Community of HiAP Professionals). "It is context-specific," and it can get started in a variety of ways, such as addressing an issue identified as part of a state's health improvement process that outlines efforts to promote health or taking on disparities identified in the population.

Origins

Tennessee implemented a HiAP initiative called the Livability Collaborative in 2015 when the health department invited staff from four state agencies to meet—a group that has since grown to include representatives of twenty-four state agencies, departments, and commissions. "The idea was that if we can just get everyone together in a room and meet regularly and talk about what we do, programs, grants—we could identify opportunities for collaboration," says Dr. John Vick, director of the Office of Primary Prevention within the Tennessee Department of Health. Since that initial effort at breaking down barriers, says Vick, awareness of the benefits of partnering has grown. During bimonthly meetings, attendees present on various initiatives to garner feedback or simply broaden awareness by others in state government. Participation is voluntary, and the program is often described as having grown organically.

Tennessee's moniker reflects the goal of all participants contributing to greater livability and working better together, says Vick. Leslie Meehan, former director of the Office of Primary Prevention, described the effort as "examining ways to work more efficiently and effectively within state government to ensure an improved quality of life. . . . We define livability as the intersection of all of our missions . . . transportation, economic development, health, education, arts, recreation, housing, and food."[4] She identifies goals including coordination of services that enables a resident seeking health resources to simultaneously access food, housing, and transit resources, if needed.[5]

Meehan is a transportation planner by background, reflecting the high priority the state places on a healthy built environment, including opportunities for walking and bicycling and access to parks, trails, and playgrounds. The state has seven Healthy Development Coordinators in regional health departments across the state, working primarily in rural areas to support local initiatives on community design-related issues such as zoning, parks, recreation, and transportation—"making sure health has a seat at the table when decisions are being made," says Shannon Velasquez, Built Environment coordinator with the Office of Primary Prevention.

Vick notes that any agency that impacts the built environment is part of the Livability Collaborative, and even though they are technically separate programs, they complement one another. A typical day in the life of a Healthy Development Coordinator might, for example, involve working with city planners, Metropolitan Planning Organization staff, Department of Transportation officials, and the local transit authority to redesign a four-lane highway that lacks sidewalks to be safer and more hospitable for pedestrians.

Outcomes

The state has developed several initiatives as part of its HiAP program, including the Tennessee Ambassador League Institute, a training program to prepare front-line staff in multiple state departments to serve as leaders in cross-sector collaboration. It has also developed a set of livability indicators and potential action steps facilitated by the group's connections and understanding of sister departments' priorities. The indicators were developed in partnership with East Tennessee State University's Center for Rural Health Research, which merged its own health care access indicators project with that of the Livability Collaborative to eliminate duplication of efforts. The center contributes to the effort through its core funding.

Additional examples of how the program increases efficiency and reduces duplication: Since both the state transportation agency and the environment and conservation department—in charge of state parks, greenways, and trails—participate in the group, connections are in place for them to align projects and proposals. And new opportunities arise to incorporate health benefits into other departments' funding streams. For example, the state is considering using some funding from human services to provide food and housing for pregnant mothers as a primary prevention strategy for improving birth outcomes. "They have the funding, we have the idea," says Vick. "It opens a lot of opportunities for us to fund work we might not be able to otherwise."

Tennessee evaluated the Livability Collaborative in 2019 based on surveys and interviews with all member agencies in order to assess changes in collaboration, data coordination, and policies, plus opportunities for improvement.[6] The evaluation concluded that the effort was achieving its goals, with relationships built through networking, discussions at meetings, and greater awareness that the work of other agencies was key to success, leading to a stronger sense of shared purpose. Among other impacts identified, four agencies created new assessments or analyses related to livability, four agencies aligned their funding opportunities with each other, and three agencies created new staff positions or changed existing positions to encourage cross-sector work.[7]

Vick says that the biggest challenges to implementing Tennessee's program are demonstrating to some partnering departments that participation is worth their time and the lack of a full-time person solely dedicated to this effort. Kerry Wyss, director of environmental health at ASTHO, notes that another challenge is assuring partners that collaboration is not extra work—but rather is beneficial to an employee's current mission and the work they are already doing.

Keys to Success

What is the incentive or motivation for employees to work across departments, or what might even be described as beyond their mandates? Vick and

Velasquez believe that as administrators saw the value in multiagency col-laboration, their support for this approach filtered down and became part of the culture. Vick notes the importance of middle- to high-level manage-ment joining this effort, having heard this message from their leadership, and of including people who see the value in this approach to become cham-pions within their own organizations. And, Vick says, as public health has become more focused on primary prevention and social drivers of health, there is a growing understanding that "we have to work with others—that's the only way we're going to make an impact."

HiAP structures vary, and structure can affect funding. Vick says the lack of a dedicated funding stream for Tennessee's voluntary program requires creativity. Tennessee has made use of fellows from the governor's office and academic partnerships to provide additional support and coordi-nation. Additionally, the state created and funded its built environment program, given the need for cross-sector assistance with the many decisions made on these issues at the local level. Wyss notes that where efforts are not funded, the key to institutionalizing them is to show that by working to-gether, the group is leveraging resources—which she believes many groups are doing successfully—and integrating some HiAP work into what is al-ready taking place.

COLORADO'S HIAP PROGRAM

Colorado's HiAP focus has long-ago roots in a structure that is very unusual in the United States: The Colorado Department of Public Health and En-vironment (CDPHE) combines public health and environmental health in one agency. A history of the department notes that environmental con-cerns, including naturally occurring radioactivity and the impacts of min-ing, influenced the formation of the agency. Unlike many other states, Colorado understood early the environment's impact on public health, which is reflected in the agency's organization.[8] Accordingly, the programs that CDPHE administers range from chronic disease prevention and con-trol of infectious diseases to air and water quality protection, hazardous and solid waste management, and pollution prevention.

This groundwork helped lead to passage, in 2008, of the Colorado Pub-lic Health Act, which espouses a proactive and community-focused ap-proach. It requires assessments to be carried out in order to understand the health of communities, state and local public health improvement plans to be developed based on the assessments, and local communities to be involved in efforts to improve health.[9] The Office of Public Health Practice, Planning, and Local Partnerships assists with implementation of these activities.

The state's environmental health work is supported by numerous organizations, including the Colorado Society for Public Health Education and Colorado Directors of Environmental Health, all of which come together under the Public Health Alliance of Colorado. Recent but also relevant to the all-important environmental health education component of HiAP: CDPHE's 2023–2026 strategic plan includes the goal to "partner with the Colorado School of Public Health and other institutes of higher learning to become an Academic Health Department." That refers to a partnership between a university department and a public health agency that aims to strengthen research, practice, and teaching, with each informing the work of the other.

Origins

Staff from CDPHE's Office of Health Equity (COHE) initiated the HiAP program with the goal of incorporating health in all decision-making across state agencies while increasing equity by focusing on social (upstream) determinants of health. This was also unusual because it was a bottom-up rather than top-down effort. Another uncommon aspect is the use of an equity lens rather than a health lens. This perspective is meant "to prevent unintentionally creating wider health disparities," according to an analysis by the Public Health Accreditation Board.[10] A case study by the Public Health National Center for Innovations (PHNCI) and the National Opinion Research Center (NORC) of the University of Chicago notes that COHE staff educated themselves by reviewing literature and talking with other state agencies doing HiAP work. Learning that many other states initiate HiAP via a high-level mandate, which Colorado did not have, they saw the importance of coordinating across agencies and stakeholders to overcome "language and communication barriers between government and community partners, siloed state government, and a lack of understanding of how to advance equity, among other factors."[11]

Activities the agency has carried out include developing an Equity Alliance that encompasses broad and both traditional and nontraditional partnerships ranging from the Denver Indian Family Resource Center to Enterprise Community Partners (a national developer of affordable housing) to most state agencies, with buy-in from the governor. It held a statewide Equity Forum with opportunities for local and state leaders to network across fields like transportation, urban planning, and criminal justice. The agency developed a curriculum and workshops to teach community members how to find data and use it in projects and an action guide linking data with recommended actions. And it gives grants to help recipients develop policy changes.[12] COHE is on the steering committees for several long-range state planning efforts.

As in Tennessee, the built environment is a major area of focus for Colorado's HiAP work. The built environment team works across state agencies and community partners to incorporate health—for example, supporting local governments to implement land use and zoning policies that will address inequities and promote health, and working with community partners to increase access to healthy food and affordable, safe housing. Another focus is climate change, with the Colorado Interagency Climate Team addressing mitigation and adaptation across a dozen state agencies. The team also works with the Governor's Environment and Renewables Cabinet Working Group and university research and extension partners, from the Cooperative Institute for Research in Environmental Sciences at the University of Colorado Boulder to the Climate Adaptation Partnership at Colorado State University.[13]

Outcomes

In 2023, the national Public Health Accreditation Board highlighted Colorado's work in this area, noting that "the environment in which people live, work, and learn has a profound impact on health, but policies and programs that shape environments generally fall outside the jurisdiction of health agencies."[14] It cites COHE's accomplishments while describing challenges that include the difficulty of hiring a social epidemiologist to help identify root causes of inequity, as this type of professional needs to have an unusual background combining sociology, epidemiology, and quantitative methods. And it has sometimes been challenging to persuade staff who are not from health agencies to engage, due to traditional concepts of silos.

When PHNCI and NORC of the University of Chicago analyzed Colorado's HiAP program in 2019, they found that it was succeeding in strengthening cross-sector relationships, with significant collaboration on projects. Participants in workshops felt positive about them. They noted that the Equity Alliance has developed a community engagement policy and a pilot project in which multiple state agencies work together to expand investments in a designated community. COHE is collecting data in order to measure the impact of HiAP efforts on efficiencies and cost savings.

The state's HiAP work spans the state and local levels. William Mundo of the University of Colorado Anschutz Medical Campus and colleagues examined eight municipalities in Colorado to understand HiAP at the local level.[15] They found that successful implementation of HiAP was (as always!) tied to education about the distinction between direct health care and population health and about the impacts of social determinants of health. This was important in both local health departments (LHDs) and other government departments. Also helpful is an understanding of how to efficiently implement HiAP with limited resources and staff. One state policy expert noted that "sending folks to the table who are not systems and policy thinkers limits their ability to see the fuller picture of cause and effect, often leading to unintended consequences." Some LHDs designated one staff member as the HiAP point person, with the expectation that they would become the HiAP expert and ambassador for that agency; such "role clarity" could help lead to more success. Challenges identified included lack of funding or overly restricted funding, which "restricts [LHDs'] ability to be innovative." Some LHDs felt positive about HiAP but did not know how to implement it due to lack of guidance from the state.

What specific strategies did LHDs in Colorado use to successfully implement HiAP? Data sharing was identified as an important tool: One department shared a public health data system with health care partners. Additionally, three LHDs worked together on the Thriving Colorado community dashboard to share information. Some LHDs helped community partners with grant writing or even operated as fiscal agents for smaller partner organizations that lacked that capacity. Several interviewees regularly attended meetings of agencies that do work that impacts health, even when the LHD staff member did not have a specific matter that was relevant to the meetings at that time. Interviewees also mentioned the importance of tracking how HiAP impacts policy development.

The study authors recommend that the state develop a standard framework for developing and evaluating progress, given the variation from one municipality to another in size, staffing, expertise, etc. Second, it would be helpful for Colorado LHDs to be allotted more time and funds for HiAP so that they do not need to use discretionary funds for these activities.

Keys to Success

The PHNCI/NORC case study identified several keys to COHE's success:

- The state ensures agency-level support for innovative approaches. A culture of innovation at COHE includes an annual innovations award program and strong support for innovation from CDPHE's top leadership.
- Staff exercised patience and persistence in building relationships. At the start, COHE staff found it challenging to develop relationships with those from other sectors. But over time, the work to build relationships led to collaboration and momentum became self-sustaining.
- Staff explained terms—for example, how health is broader than health care.
- COHE staff worked to ensure cross-sectoral participation. At times, due to space limitations, they had to limit attendees from the public health sector in order to leave room for those from other sectors; they made sure to cogently explain this. Similarly, they addressed the challenge of explaining to those from outside the public health sector why they should participate.

༄

How are Tennessee's and Colorado's experiences relevant to other states? Again, much depends on the state's culture and priorities. For example, Caliornia's HiAP program addresses both current and historical inequities.[16] Florida initially took on algae growth on waterways as part of a "health and prosperity" focus.[17] In general, these efforts seem to be on the increase. A contributing factor, according to Wyss, is a COVID-era recognition of the importance of upstream contributors to health, health equity, and partnerships that include "data sharing across the board" as necessary to build trust and reach communities on issues such as immunization.

Governments use a range of frameworks. State HiAP programs are more likely than local initiatives to include an organizing structure such as a task force, due to the larger number of partners being brought together.[18] Vermont's HiAP Task Force, for example, was established by an executive order signed by the governor in 2015 and sits at the level of state cabinet agencies. The goal is "to identify strategies to integrate health considerations into all state programs and policies and promote better health outcomes through interagency partnership," while also advancing a host of related goals such as protecting agricultural lands, planning sustainable communities, and addressing climate change.[19] Structures may also change over time. California's HiAP program, initiated with an executive order signed by the governor in 2010, was successful enough that in 2016 it was elevated to sit under the umbrella of a cabinet-level committee.[20]

HiAP efforts can intersect with state health improvement plans (SHIPs) and benefit from this connection. ASTHO found that cross-sector/HiAP work is often funded through activities related to SHIP and state health planning processes, which use state partnerships to develop and implement a plan to address health challenges.[21] An ASTHO report notes that since HiAP strategies "directly relate" to the actions involved in SHIP planning— both are collaborative and seek to improve health and equity—some states have used this planning process to advance cross-sector work.[22] Tennessee's Livability Collaborative serves as a key partner in developing metrics and recommendations for the state's SHIP.[23]

Structural choices include whether a law, executive order, or resolution brings the program into existence. A model in which HiAP is established through a law or executive order might provide more continuity but require more upfront effort to develop buy-in from agency staff, since they are responding to a mandate rather than volunteering. Wyss notes that a more formal mandate could help make a HiAP effort sustainable but could also create more restrictions. But she also works with informal groups that are very successful. "We've seen both, and there are benefits to both ways," she says. ChangeLab Solutions, a nonprofit organization that uses law and policy to advance health equity, offers a model HiAP ordinance, a resolution, and a general plan. The organization notes that the three models "offer options for communities at different stages of readiness" and can be adapted to meet a community's needs.[24]

Studies back up the idea that one size does not fit all. For example, one exploration of health equity-focused HiAP efforts, by Peter Jacobson, a professor of health law and policy at the University of Michigan, found that while a formal legal mandate is useful, it is not necessary, and steps forward were accomplished through "informal social networks that expanded over time." Research by Jacobson and a colleague noted that implementation is a long process, and political support is a prerequisite.[25] They found that HiAP efforts started small, were based on interpersonal relationships, and sometimes "demonstrated proof of concept to other governmental agencies and community organizations," leading to joint efforts in areas such as grant-making.[26]

The Public Health Accreditation Board, in its analysis of Colorado's HiAP program, advises, "Don't shy away from testing simultaneous activities, even if all the answers aren't clear up front. It sometimes works better to 'build the plane while flying.'" While a state or other jurisdiction may not be ready or able to adopt a full HiAP program, the board notes, they could adopt or adapt elements of HiAP to a local context. They also emphasize, again, the importance of hiring "dedicated staff who are familiar with managing systems-level change and cross-disciplinary collaboration."[27]

HiAP resources include many guidance documents available from organizations such as ASTHO and NACCHO. The Kansas Health Institute developed a HiAP checklist that clearly and succinctly lays out considerations and steps for any organization embarking on a HiAP effort. Figure 6-1 is a one-page summary of this approach, and figure 6-2 provides a checklist of social, economic, and environmental conditions that a proposal has the potential to impact. Along with information, federal grants have been available to support these efforts.

Health Impact Checklist

Summary Page

Proposal Name:		
Key Points of Proposal:		
Impacted Social, Economic and Environmental Conditions:	Potential Health Impacts:	
Impacted Population(s):	Recommendations:	
Entity Completing the HI-C:	Entity Receiving the HI-C:	Completion Date:

FIGURE 6-1. Health Impact Checklist Summary Page. (*Source:* Kansas Health Institute)

Health Impact Checklist

Section 1: General Information

1. Name of proposal:

2. Provide a short summary of the key points of the proposal, including expected outcomes if specified in the proposal.

3. Which of the following social, economic and environmental conditions (determinants of health) does the proposal have the greatest potential to impact? (Check at least three.)

Social, Economic and Environmental Conditions		
Economic Stability	**Neighborhood & Physical Environment**	**Education**
__Employment	__Housing Quality	__Early Childhood Education and Development
__Income	__Transportation	__High School Graduation
__Housing Instability/Homelessness	__Environmental Conditions (e.g., water, air and soil quality)	__Higher Education
__Food Insecurity	__Access to Healthy Food	__Language
__Poverty	__Safety	__Literacy
__Other	__Other	__Other
__Other	__Other	__Other
Community and Social Context	**Health and Health Care**	
__Social Participation	__Health Coverage	*Note: The number of social,*
__Discrimination	__Provider Availability	*economic or environmental*
__Toxic Stress	__Access to Health Care	*conditions examined could*
__Social Isolation	__Access to Behavioral Health Services	*depend on available resources, stakeholder*
__Incarceration	__Quality of Care	*interest and timeline. After examining three, additional*
__Other	__Other	*conditions may be examined*
__Other	__Other	*further.*

FIGURE 6-2. Health Impact Checklist General Information section. (*Source:* Kansas Health Institute)

If some of the findings and recommendations in this chapter seem rather general, that is likely due to a lack of clear metrics for measuring HiAP outcomes. To address that gap, in 2024 ASTHO and NACCHO, with funding from CDC, developed an evaluation tool for state and local governments. It uses the seven HiAP implementation strategies and ASTHO's four implementation phases of HiAP listed at the beginning of this chapter as a framework.[28]

Similarly, Vermont has developed a Total Health Expenditure Analysis tool, which it describes as the only effort of its kind in the country. The tool aims to quantify health investments by nonhealth sectors, in order to "rebalance" health spending among clinical care and other areas of spending that affect health, such as access to healthy food or safe transportation. "What we spend on health is disproportionate to the things that make us healthy," according to an explanation of the project. "Health care is only a small contributor to our health but accounts for a large amount of what we spend." By illuminating how activities in different areas affect health and well-being, this project "seeks to transform what and how we spend on population-level health, and by doing so, become a national model," according to the state's health department.[29] The idea is to "shift the paradigm from a focus on healthcare to health" and better align spending with benefits to health. This effort complements related state actions to control health care costs while improving residents' health.

Vermont's unique tool illustrates both how quickly HiAP efforts are moving forward in different states and municipalities and the breadth and creativity of various approaches. It will be fascinating to see whether and how these many different paths begin to align, and how well various approaches work in protecting and improving environmental health.

While Health in All Policies often aims to address health disparities, the goals go beyond that. "You're using data and partnerships essentially to drive change . . . for elders, children, pregnant women," says Sandra Whitehead of George Washington University and the Society of Practitioners of Health Impact Assessment. "It's everyone who breathes air or drinks water."

SEVEN

The Need for Federal Guidance

COVID-19 Mitigation in Schools

The COVID-19 pandemic brought a new and different kind of pesticide issue to my family. In February 2021, I received the return-to-school plan from my younger son's school. It included a three-page table describing where and how often (mostly hourly or after every use of a doorknob or light switch) an EPA-registered disinfectant would be applied in the school building via spray bottle or wipe, including in classrooms and common areas.

Numerous problems jumped out at me—and at other parents in the community. Disinfectants are regulated as pesticides by the EPA, and requirements of other pesticides, such as the mandate to follow the pesticide label, apply to disinfectants too. This product's label, which I requested from school staff, read "Keep out of reach of children." Yet the plan stated that staff would disinfect tables before and after students ate in the classroom, while they were in the classroom. It was a quaternary ammonium product, which can cause asthma symptoms, new onset asthma, contact dermatitis, and eye injuries; it can even disrupt critical cellular pathways.[1] The product carried the "danger" warning—a high alert level. It was not on the EPA's list of safer disinfectants. And there didn't seem to be any state or local policy or guidance on this issue.

ORIGINS

My son's school was not alone in its plan to address a risky virus by using disinfectants that pose health risks themselves. At that time, both US and global public health organizations were sending conflicting messages about how COVID-19 was transmitted. According to research by a large group of scientists from around the world, led by Jose L. Jimenez of the University of Colorado Boulder and Linsey C. Marr of Virginia Tech, at the start of the pandemic, public health organizations stated that transmission of the virus occurred via large droplets that fell to the ground and through touching contaminated surfaces. This contrasted with many scientists, who countered that aerosol (or airborne) inhalation was a significant component of transmission.[2]

In September 2020, the CDC posted on its website an acknowledgment of COVID's airborne transmission. But it took that message down a few days later. When the agency acknowledged the importance of aerosol transmission in May 2021, it used unclear language that continued to give the impression that large droplets and surfaces were the primary concern for transmission—such that regular disinfecting of surfaces was called for.[3] The World Health Organization's recognition of airborne transmission was similarly delayed. Jimenez, Marr, and their colleagues cite a number of possible explanations for this, ranging from a conceptual mistake based on traditional public health tenets, to groupthink, to concern about costs of actions to address aerosol transmission.

According to the authors, the slow acceptance of airborne transmission "contributed to a suboptimal control of the pandemic." Indeed, rather than focusing on improving ventilation and filtration systems, along with outdoor activities for children, schools overused potentially harmful disinfectants.[4] And they spent a portion of the billions of dollars in federal COVID-19 relief funds on unhelpful items such as disposable gowns and plexiglass barriers. These items pose their own environmental, and thus public health, risks. For example, the pandemic saw a huge rise in solid waste, which can cause harmful air emissions during transportation and disposal. Manufacturing of items that were unneeded can cause many types of pollution and toxic emissions when accounting for their full life cycle, which begins with materials extraction.

Much of the waste generated during COVID was plastic, which breaks down into microplastics—fragments that are smaller than five millimeters—and nanoplastics, extremely small plastic particles that result from breakdown of plastic products. Both are increasingly linked with a wide range of health concerns and are in fact becoming one of public health's biggest concerns and challenges. As just one example, a March 2024 study published in the *New England Journal of Medicine* identifies microplastics as a possible risk factor for heart disease.[5] Another paper, by Minghui Li of Chongqing University in China and colleagues, describes potential environmental and health impacts of the disposable face masks worn during COVID in terms of the degradation of their plastic polymers, such as polystyrene, that can be transported long distances and ingested by fish, which are then eaten by people. Li and colleagues state that the plastic particles in disposable face masks—which can be absorbed by skin, inhaled, or ingested—"could cause gastrointestinal toxicity, pulmonary toxicity, neurotoxicity, hepatotoxicity [injury to the liver], cardiovascular toxicity, kidney toxicity, skin toxicity, and reproductive toxicity."[6]

While some waste was inevitable, it could have been reduced if the government had communicated priorities more clearly. It is particularly unfortunate that little attention was paid to an effective solution with few downsides: improving ventilation and air filtration in schools. Many school buildings are old and poorly maintained, with leaks and mold, or are contaminated with lead, asbestos, or PCBs. Many have inadequate air flow because their heating, ventilation, and air-conditioning (HVAC) systems are outdated or the windows do not work properly. This can lead to carbon dioxide levels rising, causing students to feel sleepy and have trouble concentrating, and to indoor contaminants becoming more concentrated. Improved filtration is also needed, particularly in areas where outdoor air quality is poor due to industrial or vehicle emissions or smoke from wildfires and is brought indoors either through the HVAC system or via open windows. Both air pollution and hot days are increasing around the country due to climate change.

These affect school indoor air quality and comfort, as well as student health and academic performance. Poor indoor air quality in schools leads to more sick days taken by students and staff and can contribute to illnesses such as asthma. According to *Education Week*, "A wide body of academic research has shown that lawmakers' inability to maintain school buildings has led to lower academic outcomes for students and a lower well-being for the teachers and administrators who spend long periods of time in school buildings."[7] Figure 7-1 identifies needed updates or replacements to HVAC and

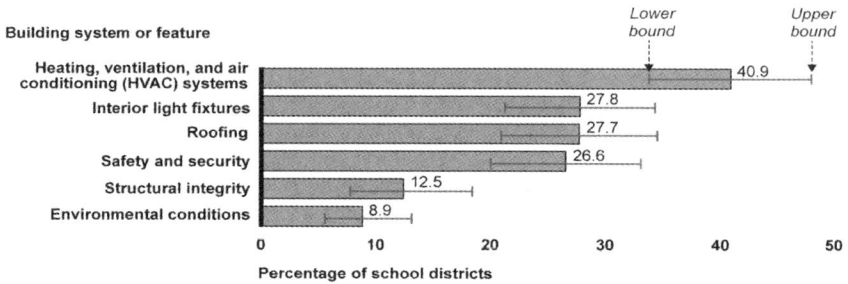

FIGURE 7-1. Estimated percentage of public school districts in which at least half the schools need updates or replacements of selected school building systems and features. (Source: US Government Accountability Office report, "K-12 Education: School Districts Frequently Identified Multiple Building Systems Needing Updates or Replacement," June 4, 2020).

other physical systems in public school buildings, as reported in a June 2020 US Government Accountability Office report.[8] In this context of extreme neglect of building systems, prioritizing the disinfection of surfaces—even if that was an effective way to slow disease transmission, which it was not—comes across like putting lipstick on a pig.

The Elementary and Secondary School Emergency Relief (ESSER) Fund did not correct this situation. Congress created ESSER to address impacts of COVID-19 on schools, giving them $190 billion in emergency funding. As described in a May 2021 US Department of Education publication, ESSER (and related Governor's Emergency Education Relief program) funds could be used for a wide range of activities, primarily focused on responding to students' social, emotional, and academic needs, advancing educational equity, and reopening schools. They also could be used for health and safety actions "such as improving ventilation and implementing prevention strategies that are, to the extent practicable, consistent with the Centers for Disease Control and Prevention (CDC) guidance."[9]

The document delineates twenty possible areas of expenditures (offered as guidance, and not meant to be comprehensive). The list includes the following related specifically to environmental health and building operations in schools: staff training on sanitation and minimizing the spread of infectious disease; purchasing supplies to sanitize and clean buildings and facilities; school facility repairs and improvements to enable operation of schools to reduce risk of virus transmission and exposure to environmental health hazards; and inspection, repair, replacement, and upgrade projects to improve indoor air quality in schools, including HVAC systems and air filtering/cleaning. In prioritizing expenditures of the funds, schools "should consider how to use those funds to safely reopen schools for full-time instruction . . . maintain safe in-person operations, advance educational equity, and build capacity."[10] This language is notably vague, and it is unclear how governors, mayors, school superintendents, and principals—who generally lack environmental health knowledge—might make sense of it.

In May 2022, the National Council of State Legislatures reported on school districts' use of ESSER funds, noting that the money is "intended to be extremely flexible, with 90% spent at the discretion of local school districts." Most of the funding (about 29 percent) was spent on academic interventions; facility upgrades made up 17.4 percent of spending; technology made up 10 percent; and combined spending on COVID mitigation measures and student mental health services made up 6.6 percent.[11]

According to Dr. Joseph Allen of Harvard's public health school and Dr. Celine Gounder of NYU Grossman School of Medicine, while the congressional funding was sufficient to upgrade school infrastructure, none of the funding bills included "any specific guidance or standards for schools to follow, so it [was] very confusing for school districts." They recommended that federal teams assist in creating indoor air quality, water quality, and energy efficiency dashboards to improve accountability and transparency—and to simultaneously benefit pandemic resilience, student and staff resilience, and climate resilience.[12] This did not take place (although financial support to improve school indoor air quality expanded a few years later, especially via the federal infrastructure law). Jimenez, Marr, and colleagues note that, overall, officials "seemed content to promote measures that only require personal responsibility, such as handwashing, and were much more reluctant to explain airborne transmission clearly as it would require costly actions on their part, for example, to improve ventilation and filtration in public buildings."

An article in *Chemical & Engineering News* states that after health officials finally acknowledged that COVID-19 was transmitted mainly through the air, the CDC recommended increasing ventilation in buildings but did not offer specific guidance about how to accomplish that for several more years. "In fact," notes this analysis, it was not until after the United States "ended its COVID-19 public health emergency in May 2023 that the CDC provided a precise ventilation target" identifying recommended air changes per hour. The analysis also notes that most schools could not meet that target, given infrastructure limitations.[13]

CONTRIBUTORS TO POOR OUTCOMES

An important factor in the confused and ineffective environmental health response to COVID-19 in schools is that public health in the United States is primarily regulated by state government—and in this novel situation, federal guidance was needed but was largely absent or unclear.

State public health responsibilities typically include preparing for emergencies, investigating disease outbreaks, abating "nuisances" (related to air quality, for example), and carrying out toxicology activities such as assessing chemical or biological risks. In a public health emergency, states also possess broad public health police powers, defined as "the inherent power of a government to exercise reasonable control over persons and property within its jurisdiction in the interest of the general security, health, safety, morals, and welfare except where legally prohibited [that is, clearly preserved for the federal government]."[14] These powers vary but often include the authority to issue stay-at-home orders, limit gatherings, and enact quarantines. So, during COVID-19, it was governors, not the president, who took actions such as mandating masks.

At the start of the pandemic, with the Trump administration focused on efforts such as vaccine development, state responses veered in a range of directions and became politicized. The disjointed responses of states continued under President Biden. Indeed, the lack of a unified response was baked into the cake of environmental health regulation. Indoor air quality is mostly unregulated by the federal government. Occupational safety and health protections for teachers and other school staff under federal or state OSHA programs do not ensure a healthy indoor environment or use of healthy products, due to shortcomings in that area of policy. Meanwhile, federal guidance on various aspects of indoor air quality is spread across agencies. The EPA and Department of Energy provide information about indoor air quality in buildings, including schools. EPA regulates disinfectants under the federal pesticide law, but during COVID-19, many found its guidance on choosing safer disinfectants confusing.

Healthy homes expert David Jacobs explains why there has never been more than minimal regulation of the indoor environment, whereas the Clean Air Act extensively regulates outdoor air quality. Indoors, he writes, there is not the same feeling of a "commons" that would create a sense of public responsibility. Instead, indoor air "sits within the enclosed space of one's own home or another discrete building." Additionally, a polluter of indoor air typically cannot be easily identified and held responsible for remediation. This is in part because of the many different personnel involved in building design and upkeep, from architects and designers to employers, custodians, and occupants. In the absence of an identifiable party that can be responsible for correcting problems, "there has been less public support to demand mandates to control indoor pollution."[15]

Some environmental health functions—including indoor air quality—are even left to the local level of government. People spend the vast majority of their time indoors, and many of these hours are spent in settings like school and offices, where their presence is mandatory. So, a safe and healthy environment in schools, where children—one of the most important, yet vulnerable, groups in our society—spend much of their time is mainly the responsibility of state and local officials. This scenario presented many challenges during COVID-19.

A major obstacle was (and continues to be) declining funding. Dr. Megan Wallace and Dr. Joshua Sharfstein describe how public health in the U.S. has been chronically underfunded: "In addition to gaps in support of specific federal health efforts such as pandemic preparedness, state government funding for public health has stagnated, with no growth occurring between 2008 and 2018."[16] They note that as part of a national shortage of public health workers, most public health departments lack staff "in specialized roles that are critical to the delivery of essential public health services," such as community health workers, epidemiologists, and statisticians. They contrast the poverty-stricken public health system with the well-endowed health care sector, noting that, before COVID, funds for public health constituted less than 3 percent of health care expenditures in the United States, while Congress provided $178 billion for the health care system. According to the Trust for America's Health, COVID-19 emergency funding failed to address "structural weaknesses" in the country's public health system, including "antiquated data systems," insufficient laboratory capacity, and communications challenges—all of which require both increased and stable funding.[17]

So, why is public health chronically underfunded? In part, it is because the field is subject to a cycle of "panic and neglect."[18] It is easy not to notice public health, which works to prevent illness, when it is doing its job, making it a target for budget and staffing cuts—until a new crisis creates panic, and underfunded and understaffed agencies are again overwhelmed with meeting the demands of the moment.

Another challenge for state and local decision-makers during COVID-19 was inadequate data provision by CDC, which reduced the effectiveness of federal communication and guidance. Although states are the main government entities responsible for protecting public health, it was federal public health agencies, with their access to comprehensive data and ability to mandate some types of data collection, that had overall responsibility for collecting and analyzing COVID-19 data. CDC is the "main assessment and epidemiologic unit for the country" and provides technical assistance to states and localities; within CDC, the National Center for Health Statistics "is the main authority for collecting, analyzing, and disseminating health data," according to the Institute of Medicine (now the National Academy of Medicine).[19]

However, due to factors including outmoded data systems and concerns about misinterpretation of information, CDC failed to provide refined, specific statistics.[20] This shortcoming at the federal level, and also among some states, was seen as hampering efforts on the ground to be more "strategic" with interventions and "identify targeted measures that could stem the spread of SARS-CoV-2 without full-scale lockdowns," according to an article in *Science* dramatically titled "Data Secrecy Is Crippling Attempts to Slow COVID-19's Spread in U.S., Epidemiologists Warn."[21] More refined statistics could have helped in decision-making about mitigation efforts in schools. The *Science* article describes how some clinics in California carried out their own research in order to identify areas of outbreaks "both geographically and in terms of setting." It quotes one physician at a community health center as noting that a lack of neighborhood-level intelligence for public health outreach results in "a one-size-fits-all solution that might exacerbate the problem."

In fact, some groups of experts formed their own efforts to analyze and communicate COVID data. Johns Hopkins University launched its Pandemic Data Initiative to help compensate for government shortfalls. Each state reports demographic information related to COVID policies in schools differently "because there are no federal standards for such reporting," according to an article about the initiative written by staff of the university. The data that the Hopkins group developed was more refined than what had previously been provided to school decision-makers. Government data, by contrast, was aggregated and "telling a very homogeneous view of the way the outbreak was manifesting in communities," said Beth Blauer, a leader of the effort, echoing some of the complaints from California neighborhoods. "We need data to come from state and local communities and also the federal government into schools" to help them navigate difficult decisions, including physical distancing and mask mandates.[22]

Finally, due to the environment–health disconnect that begins at the federal level of government, then is often replicated at the state and local levels, many state and local health department staff—and certainly school district staff—may lack sufficient knowledge about ventilation, filtration, and safe and effective cleaning and disinfecting. These aspects of a healthy indoor environment are always important and were especially so during the pandemic.

These shortcomings point to what is needed for next time. And we can be certain of numerous next times, especially as warmer temperatures fueled by climate change push disease-carrying insects into new locations, heat up school buildings, and contribute to more air pollution.

LESSONS FOR THE FUTURE

What needs to happen? For state and local governments to be well-informed public health decision-makers in these situations, federal agencies must have the most up-to-date tools to collect, share, and communicate health data—and they must then provide clear guidance.

S. E. Galaitsi and colleagues, all with the US Army Corps of Engineers, make a few specific recommendations, some of which are already being implemented: identify a centrally recognized authority to issue standards for all data-reporting entities to follow; be responsive to the needs of users; and, where data is imperfect or contains inconsistencies, clearly indicate this. They note that state websites that contained subsets of data specific to certain groups or settings—such as public schools and universities—were informative for those tasked with making COVID-related policy decisions. "Providing these disaggregations of data, where possible, can deepen the breadth of analysis," they write.[23]

Dr. Howard Koh, Harvard University public health professor who was previously assistant secretary for health for the US Department of Health and Human Services, called in May 2020 for the federal government to use its unique position to provide clear guidance and best practices for the states: "Only the federal government can establish standards for the country to synchronize state surveillance, establish benchmarks, monitor outcomes, disseminate best practices, and offer consistent health messages that can lead to a healthier and more informed populace."[24] Since COVID-19 affected the whole country, "explicit federal coordination of the response to and the recovery from" the pandemic was required, he continues, noting that the public was left "unnerved" by the spectacle of states competing with each other for supplies such as personal protective equipment (PPE). A unified COVID-19 response and recovery plan "could be tailored and implemented locally" in order to support states "as they apply science-based policies to their own communities."

Additionally, the data and guidance from the federal government must be "whole of government," according to Dr. Koh—involving all agencies with relevant missions. He is referring to a Health in All Policies approach in which agencies reach beyond silos to work together to maximize efficiency and improve outcomes. Next time, in addition to CDC, one can envision federal agencies including EPA, OSHA, the Department of Energy, the Department of Education, and others being involved. Their combined expertise can help to answer the following questions: What is the right way to balance using PPE such as disposable face masks for protection from infectious disease, relative to the environmental and health risks of exposure to the masks' microplastics and their solid waste challenges? What is the return on investment of various HVAC upgrades in school buildings? Since resources (supplies, money, time, energy) will always be limited, answering these questions can help balance one risk against another, or compare the benefits and risks of a possible action, in order to come up with the most useful solution.

A focus on indoor air quality will be key to preparing both for future pandemics and increased heat and air pollution due to climate change. Jimenez, Marr, and colleagues note that the understanding that arose from COVID that most respiratory diseases are transmitted at least partly via air has "major implications for the regulation and control of air quality in indoor spaces, by proper ventilation, filtration, and other means."

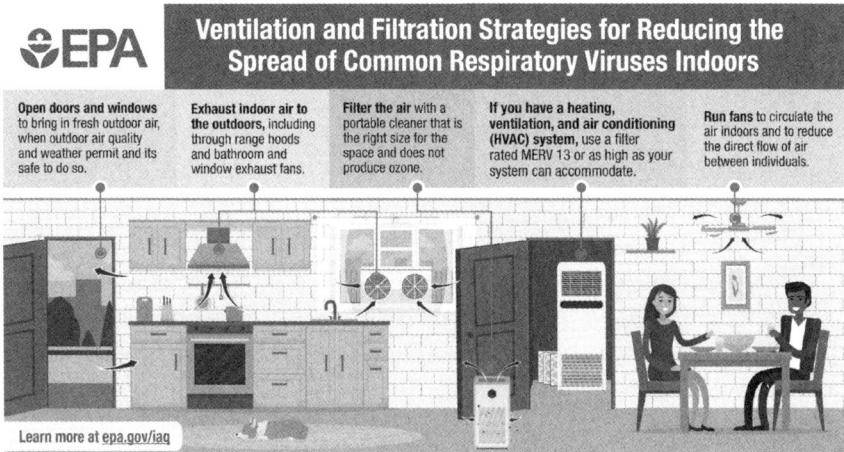

⬧EPA   Ventilation and Filtration Strategies for Reducing the Spread of Common Respiratory Viruses Indoors

Open doors and windows to bring in fresh outdoor air, when outdoor air quality and weather permit and its safe to do so.

Exhaust indoor air to the outdoors, including through range hoods and bathroom and window exhaust fans.

Filter the air with a portable cleaner that is the right size for the space and does not produce ozone.

If you have a heating, ventilation, and air conditioning (HVAC) system, use a filter rated MERV 13 or as high as your system can accommodate.

Run fans to circulate the air indoors and to reduce the direct flow of air between individuals.

Learn more at epa.gov/iaq

FIGURE 7-2. EPA graphic showing strategies to reduce indoor spread of respiratory viruses. (*Source*: US Environmental Protection Agency)

Ventilation—introducing fresh air from outside into a building, as well as moving air around within it—helps to reduce humidity and buildup of pollutants. Filtration reduces contaminants entering and circulating within a building. These are illustrated in figure 7-2.

The American Lung Association pulled together clear and streamlined recommendations for healthy schools in 2022. They are perhaps the ones that the federal government should have started with during COVID-19. The American Lung Association's report is titled *A National Asthma Public Policy Agenda—2022 Update*, but its recommendations for schools go beyond asthma to both mitigating COVID-19 and creating a healthy school environment for all. The report notes that the pandemic exposed many of the country's long-term public health challenges and that the asthma report's recommendations "are even more timely and urgent considering this global respiratory pandemic." The association urges that all educational systems "adopt and implement environmental assessment and management protocols that are based on current research and best practices," as follows:

• Develop and implement an indoor air quality (IAQ) program as detailed in the EPA's Indoor Air Quality Tools for Schools plan, which recommends low-cost actions to prevent and address most IAQ problems, to be undertaken by a team led by an IAQ coordinator.

- Strive for ventilation systems that meet the minimum guidelines of the American Society of Heating, Refrigerating and Air-Conditioning Engineers.
- Follow practices to reduce exposure to cleaning agents and disinfectants that cause or aggravate asthma, including using products certified by EPA as safer.
- Require schools, grounds, facilities, and vehicles to be tobacco-free.
- Minimize students' exposure to outdoor air pollutants on days with unhealthy levels of air pollution, including by using ventilation/filtration and other strategies to reduce exposures inside school buildings.
- Adopt zero-emission technology for school buses and policies to prevent school bus and personal car idling on school grounds.
- Develop and implement a disaster response plan that addresses exposure to indoor and outdoor pollutants (e.g., mold, wildfires), access to asthma medication, and cleaning up schools.[25]

The American Lung Association notes that school buildings face special IAQ challenges: They have four times more occupants than office buildings; possible sources of indoor air problems from many types of spaces, from gyms to cafeterias; and often tight budgets that could negatively impact upkeep or purchase of needed upgrades.[26]

Going beyond building systems and operations, COVID-19 clearly demonstrated the need to address upstream contributors to health outcomes. Chronic and common conditions like obesity were major comorbidities for severe COVID cases and death. So, in the school setting, every effort should be made to ensure that students have access to healthy food, physical education, and participation in intramural or competitive sports. Many policy decisions that affect student access to healthy food take place on the federal level, including as part of the Farm Bill package of legislation that addresses agriculture and food; others related to food and physical education are made at the state and local levels. While many schools' provision of free meals to all children during COVID-19 was a positive step, and school meals have gotten healthier overall, researchers at the Tufts University Friedman School of Nutrition Science and Policy find that one in four school meals are still of poor nutritional quality.[27] A broad Health in All Policies approach would address not just infectious diseases but the overall health of schoolchildren—which would increase their health and resilience in the face of future pandemics and other challenges.

Post-COVID, there were indications that things might be moving in the right direction. The Department of Energy and EPA awarded grants to improve IAQ in schools; the Association of State and Territorial Health Officials reported in late 2024 that Kentucky, Michigan, and Washington increased funding for public health services in their annual budgets;[28] and, in 2024, EPA released updated guidance on IAQ strategies to reduce the spread of viruses indoors. The CDC was allotted funding to modernize its data systems, although in spring 2025 that effort appeared to be jeopardized by budget and staff cuts.

In the higher education context, Joseph Allen, Harvard T.H. Chan School of Public Health professor and a major advocate for prioritizing school air quality during COVID-19, announced that his 2025 healthy buildings class, which had previously included some Harvard Graduate School of Design students, would for the first time be officially cross-listed at both schools, as well as co-taught by him and a design school professor. "There's magic when public health students and design students are in the same room," he commented. Since cross-listing courses at two or more university departments can run into an array of bureaucratic obstacles, this development is a bigger deal than one might expect.

Will these various actions set up schools to be better prepared, from an environmental health standpoint, for the next crisis? Time will tell. Next time, the federal government will need to provide clear data and guidance to state, local, and school district decision-makers. And next time should start now, with a healthy school environment prioritized in all school building construction, renovation, and operations. In order to accomplish that, all of the relevant agencies and decision-makers will need to overcome the damaging cycle of panic and neglect.

EIGHT

Cooperation Across States

Partnering to Cut Greenhouse Gases and Strengthen
Environmental Security at the Regional Level

My effort to reduce pesticide use in my neighborhood ran into many obstacles created by statewide policies. What if my fellow advocates and I had been able to partner with those in neighboring states who were making progress on this issue?

Pollution does not stop at the state line, and policy does not have to either. An approach that sits in between single-state solutions and federal policies is regional pacts. One widely touted arrangement is the Regional Greenhouse Gas Initiative (RGGI), developed by a confederation of East Coast states to reduce greenhouse gas emissions. Another is the Southeast Regional Partnership for Planning and Sustainability (SERPPAS), which is spearheaded by federal agencies and brings together environmental and military officials from six Southeastern states. It aims to sustain both natural resources and national defense assets in the region. In both cases, these partnerships have done more to protect environmental health than any of the individual states could accomplish on their own.

THE REGIONAL GREENHOUSE GAS INITIATIVE

In a cap-and-trade system, a cap is set on a pollutant, and each participant receives an allowance that represents a fraction of the overall cap. Participants can buy and sell within their allowance, which ensures that the over-all limit is not exceeded. This approach provides flexibility, since participants can choose to pay to pollute more or can pollute less and pay less. Cap-and-trade was implemented successfully by the federal government in the 1990s to address acid rain, which is formed from emissions of sulfur dioxide and nitrogen oxides, and has also been used in several other contexts. Cap-and-trade is considered a market-based mechanism that gives facilities some flexibility in reducing emissions. It is viewed as more versatile than traditional command-and-control regulation in which the government spells out the steps that facilities must take to reduce pollution.

Origins

In 2003, governors of nine Northeastern states started to discuss a regional cap-and-trade program to reduce carbon dioxide emissions, which contribute to climate change, from power plants.[1] In 2005, seven of the states agreed to implement RGGI via a memorandum of understanding. They published a model rule that the participating states could use in developing their own individual state laws governing participation in the program. Currently, eleven states are part of the cooperative effort: Connecticut, Delaware, Maine, Maryland, Massachusetts, New Hampshire, New Jersey, New York, Pennsylvania, Rhode Island, and Vermont. Virginia joined in 2020—the first Southern state to do so—then withdrew a few years later.

The participants agreed on a region-wide cap on carbon dioxide emissions from regulated power plants in the states. The cap can be thought of as a regional budget for emissions. It decreases over time in order to lower overall emissions. In every state that is part of the program, each fossil fuel–fired electric power generator with the ability to generate at least 25 megawatts buys allowances equal to its carbon dioxide emissions. The states distribute the allowances at quarterly auctions, where power plants and other entities can bid on and buy them. After an allowance is distributed, it can be held or traded, which creates a market in which allowances have a market-based value, like a currency. In fact, the auctions have been likened to a commodities market.[2]

The emissions cap went into effect on January 1, 2009. An online system tracks actions related to the allowances. Funds from sales of allowances go to the states, which invest them locally to support a clean energy economy. States have used the funds to support development of clean energy programs, energy efficiency programs, and financial assistance with energy bills for consumers.

Notre Dame law professor Bruce Huber points to two aspects of RGGI that are unusual. First, it mainly uses auctions to distribute emissions allowances. It is more typical in cap-and-trade programs, he writes, for allowances to be given to polluting entities based on their historical emissions and at no charge. But that has a big downside, which was recognized by RGGI's architects: Free allowances give existing emitters a head start and make it more difficult for new firms, like lower-emitting entities, to participate.[3]

Huber also points to restructuring (also called deregulation) of the electricity market starting in the 1990s as significant to RGGI's success. With restructuring, regional wholesale energy markets develop in order for retail suppliers to buy the energy and sell it to consumers (whereas previously one company carried out all functions). The wholesale markets were likely to lead to higher electricity rates, whether or not a state participated in RGGI. But auctions could raise revenue that would help make up for the rate increase. Additionally, since restructuring broke up the integrated functions of utilities, it opened up the opportunity for new businesses to enter the sector and participate in and benefit from the auctions.[4] This range of benefits that RGGI could provide helped the program overcome opposition, win endorsement by the states' legislators, and include use of auctions.

RGGI was conceived at a time when political divisions were less entrenched than they are today, and the program was led by a bipartisan group of governors—seven Republican and three Democratic. In fact, it was a Republican, New York Governor George Pataki, who initiated the discussions that led to RGGI. Similarly, cap-and-trade programs, including the one for acid rain, had been developed and supported by presidential administrations of both parties.[5] When Pataki invited nine fellow governors to join the bipartisan initiative, they agreed, and staff from the states' environment and energy agencies began working together to design it.

A major goal of RGGI was to increase energy efficiency. Without this objective, the problem of "leakage" would arise, meaning that less expensive but probably more polluting energy produced outside of the RGGI states could be imported into RGGI states to help meet their energy demands. That could be detrimental to meeting the initiative's goals, especially since energy in nearby states could be—and often was—produced by carbon-dioxide-intensive coal-fired power plants. Auctions, by raising funds for renewable energy development and energy efficiency programs, were expected to reduce this risk by increasing the choices of less polluting options. The relatively large number of states that participate in RGGI also lessened the chance of leakage by reducing the number of states (those that are geographically close but not part of RGGI) that could potentially offer more polluting electricity without RGGI's constraints.

The states review the program every few years. During an early review, the emissions cap was reduced because of lower-than-expected emissions— themselves due to reductions in coal plant emissions and an economic downturn that reduced overall energy consumption. Still, with an emissions cap that was higher than emissions, the allowance price succeeded in acting like a carbon tax.[6] And the emission allowances offered a new form of currency that could be, and was, invested in energy efficiency and renewable energy efforts.

Outcomes

Since RGGI's inception, the participating states have reduced annual carbon dioxide emissions from the power sector 50 percent—almost 50 percent faster than the country overall.[7] One study found that RGGI "directly caused coal and natural gas phase-outs" in the participating states by making these forms of energy production more expensive.[8] As plant owners bought allowances, their costs were incorporated into market prices and caused a shift from higher- to lower-emitting sources. Investments of auction revenue into energy efficiency and renewable energy programs further reduced emissions.

An Abt Associates analysis of RGGI's public health impacts during its first six years of implementation found that along with cutting carbon, the initiative significantly reduced hazardous air pollution such as fine particulate matter ($PM_{2.5}$), nitrogen oxides, and sulfur dioxide emitted from fossil fuel power plants—an important co-benefit of reducing carbon dioxide. This created major health benefits for residents of these states, averting hundreds of premature deaths, heart attacks, and cases of bronchitis; thousands of respiratory problems and asthma exacerbations; and "hundreds of thousands of cases of restricted activity days due to poor air quality."[9] Abt's modeling showed that neighboring non-RGGI states also enjoyed significant health benefits from RGGI due to reduced regional transport of air pollutants, as did RGGI states such as Vermont and Maine as a result of RGGI-induced emissions reductions from coal plants in Massachusetts, New Hampshire, and the western part of RGGI member New York.[10]

The Abt report notes that while emissions reductions of a small number of legacy coal plants were behind much of RGGI's initial health benefits, these benefits will continue as sectors such as transportation and buildings shift to cleaner forms of energy. It also, interestingly, proposes that energy efficiency investments funded by RGGI auction proceeds could be "strategically targeted" to reduce high fine-particulate concentrations during periods of high electricity demand. This could have significant health benefits, since "a single short-term exposure to high $PM_{2.5}$ concentrations can lead to more severe health outcomes than multiple exposures to low $PM_{2.5}$ concentrations."[11]

Dr. Frederica Perera and colleagues investigated RGGI's benefits for children's environmental health specifically, noting that assessments of the public health benefits of policies like the US Clean Air Act amendments and the Paris Climate Accord have considered "few, if any, benefits to children" or avoided costs of lifelong consequences of children's air pollution exposure. This omission has resulted "in a serious undercounting of potential health benefits for this vulnerable population," the authors write.[12] The group examined the years 2009–2014—the same that Abt analyzed—adding four outcomes related to children's $PM_{2.5}$ exposure: averted preterm births and averted cases of term low birthweight, autism spectrum disorder, and asthma. They estimated the economic value of these additional health benefits at $191 to $350 million for the study period, likely an underestimate since these impacts to children as a result of $PM_{2.5}$ exposure can have long-term consequences for them and society that are not usually accounted for.[13] These averted costs are economic benefits of RGGI. And there could be more cost savings, since this study does not look at benefits of mitigating climate change itself, which are substantial.

In terms of financial results, the RGGI states have raised $7 billion as of January 2024. Of that, 61 percent has been invested in energy efficiency and 15 percent has gone to direct financial assistance to consumers for paying energy bills. The remainder has funded development of clean and renewable energy, activities to mitigate greenhouse gas emissions, climate change adaptation, and administration. Looking at just 2022, investments from RGGI proceeds were projected to save $1.5 billion on energy bills for households and businesses.[14] One analysis calculated that RGGI resulted in $34 in net positive value per capita across the participating states during the period studied.[15]

Challenges of running RGGI include the withdrawal (and rejoining) of several states, depending on the state's political climate; determination of the proper level for the emissions cap due to changing market conditions, weather, and other factors; and a few states using RGGI revenues to address state budget holes rather than for energy efficiency, a move that was criticized by environmental groups.

Also, as noted in chapter 5's discussion of California's Community Air Protection Program, cap-and-trade programs may not benefit environmental justice areas that tend to contain a larger proportion of polluting facilities. A 2022 study found that in the RGGI states, the transition from coal to natural gas—an overall positive for reducing carbon emissions—resulted in many more generating units burning natural gas and greater total natural gas generation in EJ communities compared to other areas. Climate change and air pollution reduction policies, the authors emphasize, must go beyond aggregate emissions to address disparities in pollution burdens between EJ and non-EJ communities.[16] The RGGI states are discussing ways to address this issue.

Keys to Success

Why did this initiative develop in these particular states? Barry Rabe, a professor of public policy at the University of Michigan, attributes RGGI's success partly to these states' previous experience working together as part of national trading programs designed to reduce levels of lead in gasoline, sulfur dioxide, and nitrogen oxides. In the case of nitrogen oxides, the federal government had delegated oversight to the Northeastern states, which provided a "unique experience" that helped them develop the knowledge necessary to create RGGI.[17] Rabe also notes that environment and energy agencies in these states generally have close working relationships, which was "essential" in crafting RGGI.[18] Additionally, since state officials were free from federal mandates, they had the flexibility to balance technical and political realities, and to weigh the interests of individual states against maintaining the group pact, in order to sustain broad support.[19] Huber also notes that forming a network among the states increased the ability of state officials to connect with and draw on the resources of "an impressive array of policy experts, think tanks, advocacy groups and academic researchers" more than a single state could. The group effort also decreased the start-up costs of the effort since they shared resources.[20]

Ben Grumbles, a former Maryland environment secretary, agrees that flexibility and autonomy are keys to RGGI's success, especially when states span Democratic and Republican leadership. These ingredients, he observed in an article in *Governing* magazine, helped keep RGGI alive during political transitions, because each state develops its own plan for reducing carbon dioxide and investing revenue gained from the program.[21] While program reviews have at times revealed a risk of division along party lines, "the states were all committed to finding common ground," he writes. "Given all the debate over climate change, bipartisan environmental leadership is more important than ever before."[22]

So RGGI demonstrates the benefits of states cooperating instead of operating alone. These benefits include additional resources, economies of scale, cost-effectiveness, and reduction of leakage that could detract from the program's success.

RGGI shows that states can successfully move forward with climate policy in the absence of federal leadership. This is especially relevant since the Supreme Court in 2022 struck down the EPA's Clean Power Plan, which would have limited carbon emissions from power plants. Even when prices for allowances are low, "RGGI has still remained up and running and is contributing to the cost structure of every emitter in those states," notes Huber. "This is momentous, even if not enough to abate climate change. It demonstrates the power of policy entrepreneurs and think tanks to do something really difficult—and succeed."

What happens next? Several states beyond the RGGI states have enacted carbon pricing policies. But state policymakers agree that more needs to be done. Some are discussing setting up multistate programs to move beyond electricity to address additional sectors that contribute significantly to warming emissions, such as transportation and buildings. Figure 8-1, from the EPA, depicts the large contribution of these sectors. A group of Northeast and mid-Atlantic states, plus Washington, DC, has begun working together to explore potential regional policies to reduce transportation pollution. Known as the Transportation & Climate Initiative, the effort is led by

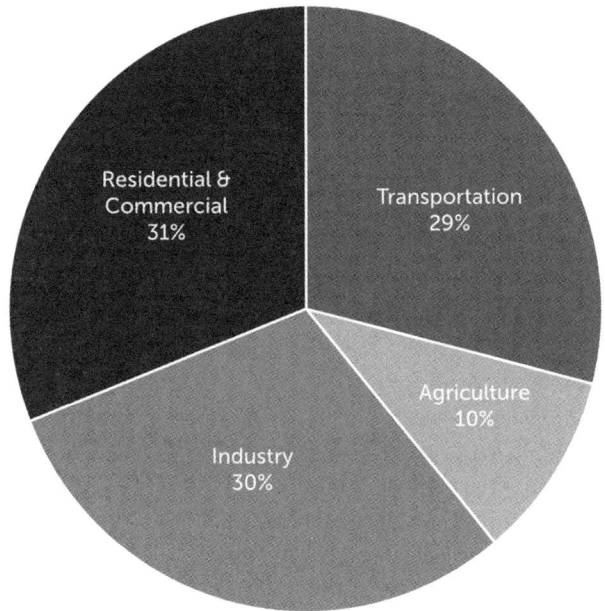

FIGURE 8-1. U.S. greenhouse gas emissions by economic sector, including electricity end-use indirect emissions, in 2022. (*Source*: U.S. Environmental Protection Agency)

Residential & Commercial 31%

Transportation 29%

Agriculture 10%

Industry 30%

the Georgetown Climate Center at Georgetown University's law school. International partnerships between US states, Canada, and other countries have also gained steam.

Barry Rabe concludes that carbon pricing can play a significant role in supporting decarbonization, but as "part of an ensemble of policies rather than a solo act." He recommends more strongly linking carbon pricing and trade policy to support decarbonization efforts and reduce leakage. When other countries put a price on carbon while the United States does not, that makes US products cheaper and reduces our incentive to include carbon in costs. This can be the case in any situation where some countries put a price on carbon and others don't. Thus, he raises the question of whether a fee could be added to goods imported from countries with a lesser climate commitment. Rabe also recommends continuing to invest program revenues in environmental sustainability programs and expanding the program to climate pollutants such as methane—a more powerful greenhouse gas than carbon dioxide— and hydrofluorocarbons that are used in air-conditioning.[23]

Meanwhile, RGGI stands as a model of cooperation across states.

THE SOUTHEAST REGIONAL PARTNERSHIP FOR PLANNING AND SUSTAINABILITY

Red-cockaded woodpeckers are protected under the Endangered Species Act, but their population was declining due to loss of the tree in which they nest: the longleaf pine. The story of the Southeast Regional Partnership for Planning and Sustainability starts with the "woodpecker wars" at Fort Bragg in North Carolina, a military installation of the US Army.

Origins

There were both woodpeckers and longleaf forest at Fort Bragg—now named Fort Liberty—and the US Fish and Wildlife Service required the army to protect the bird, which restricted its operations. Meanwhile, homeowners and developers were cutting down longleaf pines in the area. Separately, in the eastern part of North Carolina, the navy was considering siting a landing field next to a wildlife refuge for migratory birds, which could have risked their safety.

With more people moving to the Southeast, urban areas expanding, and military activities becoming more complex in the early 2000s, competition for land and natural resources went beyond the woodpeckers and their habitat. It became apparent that this regional growth would lead to loss of agricultural land, wildlife habitats, farms, forests, and fisheries, absent action to protect them. The development was also increasingly encroaching on military lands and operations. Interestingly, as available property was developed, military sites remained some of the largest and most biodiverse areas of land in the region, hosting a range of ecosystems.[24] For the military, these challenges demonstrated that developments "beyond the fence line" affected its ability to carry out its mission "inside the fence line." To address concerns such as habitat loss, effects of residential growth, and climate change impacts, the military needed to work with parties beyond its own physical boundaries.[25]

Bill Ross served as North Carolina's secretary of environment and natural resources from 2001 to 2009, during the height of the woodpecker wars. When the navy considered building a new landing field next to delicate habitat, "it occurred to me there should be a forum where the military and other parties with multiple interests in the issue could work together to find a mutually satisfactory solution," he says. "But there wasn't." The proposal got far down the road and became a challenging situation that was only resolved because the navy decided against building the field. But it led Ross—now of counsel to a North Carolina law firm—to suggest to a community engagement official at the Department of Defense that they should create a structure to resolve stakeholder concerns.

At an initial meeting in Chapel Hill in 2005, attendees explored the value of such a forum. "We wanted leaders at a high level and who had a bias toward action," says Ross. And with organizations represented that ranged widely in terms of size, resources, and staff, "we wanted rules that made everyone feel valued around the table." The group took its working principles from the book *Getting to Yes*, as illustrated in figure 8-2: Be easy on the people, hard on the issues. Focus on interests, not positions. Invent options for mutual gain. The foundational idea was to develop effective working relationships with nonconventional partners, using high-quality science and data to inform decisions. All of the participants agreed on the need for the forum.

Thus, the Southeast Regional Partnership for Planning and Sustainability was born. Its mission is "to prevent encroachment around military lands, encourage compatible resource-use decisions, and improve coordination among regions, states, communities, and military services." Objectives include sustaining and enhancing natural resources, economic resources, and national defense; strengthening environmental sustainability in the context of military base realignment (reorganization of military bases to increase efficiency) in the Southeast; and supporting these efforts through development of a "good map," a GIS tool that integrates federal, military, and state data.

The Department of Defense took on the leadership role in this "unconventional partnership" through its Readiness and Environmental Protection Integration (REPI) program. REPI enables military services to provide funds to protect areas beyond their bases, avoid land-use conflicts, and address environmental and climate change challenges. The roster of partners grew, encompassing federal agencies such as the Department of Agriculture's Forest Service and the Department of Interior's Fish and Wildlife Service; and environmental, wildlife, forestry, agricultural, and natural resources agencies of Alabama, Florida, Georgia, Mississippi, North Carolina, and South Carolina. A number of nonprofits, like The Nature Conservancy

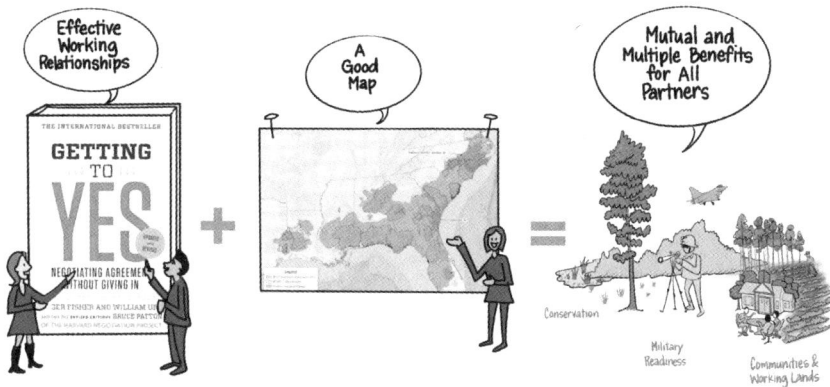

FIGURE 8-2. Graphic from SERPPAS Story Map. (Source: Kriss Wittmann, Wittmann Studios

and The Conservation Fund, also got involved. Several universities located in the Southeast, including their extension programs, did too.[26]

The Nature Conservancy explains its initial involvement in SERPPAS in terms of, again, the woodpecker: The birds fly short distances from tree to tree, so they require zones of forest that allow them to move from one to the next. The Nature Conservancy identified several key parcels that would create these corridors and fill in space between one population of woodpeckers at Fort Liberty and another at a different army facility. After identifying these properties, the conservancy was able to buy and protect them, with assistance from the army and the Fish and Wildlife Service. The woodpecker population at Fort Liberty has since recovered, longleaf pine has expanded, and this model of protection has been replicated beyond the Southeast.[27]

SERPPAS, meanwhile, has continued to play an important role in resolving conflicts and seizing opportunities. It is organized via a foundation of working groups that identify shared objectives, and each has a leader from an agency or other SERPPAS partner. The next level is a steering committee made up of senior staff of the participating state and federal agencies. The members lead the development of projects and communicate about SERPPAS within their own agencies. Finally, principals are senior leaders of participating state and federal agencies. They identify SERPPAS priorities, develop strategies to implement them, and provide overall leadership. The partnership prioritizes in-person meetings and social networking in order to build trust.[28]

As for funding, the REPI program of the Department of Defense funds a SERPPAS coordinator position and meetings of the principals and steering committee. It does so through a contractual arrangement with the Texas A&M Natural Resources Institute. The time and resources participants expend attending meetings and participating in projects is in-kind. In some situations, agencies have contributed funding for specific efforts, and some projects are supported by grant funding.

Outcomes

Since 2005, SERPPAS has been a principal actor in a number of successful initiatives that address interconnected issues. The longleaf ecosystem, discussed above, had declined from 90 million acres across the Southeast to less than 5 percent of that acreage. That this important ecosystem was concentrated in many areas on military land was challenging, because federal requirements reduced the military's ability to carry out its activities. One way to address that was to increase important ecology and habitats in areas beyond military land. For example, buffer areas were created between military bases and land that was quickly developing for residential purposes; this reduced possible noise or other complaints from neighbors while protecting military activities by keeping the land undeveloped, either as working (farm or forest) or natural land. Overall, it was beneficial for longleaf pines to grow on military bases and beyond, to provide a broader ecosystem for woodpeckers and other species that nested in or otherwise depended on the trees. SERPPAS and many partners, including Auburn University, developed the Range-Wide Conservation Plan for Longleaf Pine, which continues to be implemented more than fifteen years after its adoption.[29]

Bill Ross notes that the restoration of longleaf pine across its historic range—from southeast Virginia to east Texas—"has stopped the centuries-long decline of that forest and has it on the rise again." He emphasizes that the collective nature of the effort has generated a large group of partners and attracted significant funding: "You sometimes hear it described as the best example of a landscape-scale conservation success story in the world." Longleaf pine forests buffered many military bases as residential development moved close by—in this case, near the fence line of Fort Liberty. On the military side, Ross notes, the area that abutted the buffer was a landing zone where soldiers and equipment dropped from airplanes.

As an official stamp of the success of these efforts, in October 2024 the Fish and Wildlife Service moved the listing of the red-cockaded woodpecker down from endangered to threatened.[30] "Decades of committed recovery work and collaboration drove this remarkable story of recovery. The Service worked closely with the Departments of Agriculture and Defense, private landowners, Tribes, state agencies, businesses, utilities, and conservation groups to reach today's announcement," said Fish and Wildlife Service director Martha Williams.

Central to longleaf conservation is prescribed fire. Prescribed fire helps to restore ecosystems, improve habitats for some animals, remove invasive species and some pest populations, and reduce the risk of wildfires. In the Southeast, it expands habitat for endangered species beyond military bases and creates buffers for the bases. In line with its emphasis on unconventional partnerships, SERPPAS in 2012 brought together air quality regulators, leaders of conservation agencies, and fire practitioners to develop a comprehensive plan for prescribed fire across the SERPPAS geography. That plan continues to be implemented. Also significant was the group's influence on an EPA regulation recognizing that a carefully managed prescribed fire "is generally less likely than a wildfire to cause or contribute to an exceedance or a violation" of federal air quality standards. The working group developed a map that uses remote sensing to keep track of fire across the Southeast, which assists with decision-making. The Prescribed Fire Working Group now has more than eighty members.[31]

Building on its actions to protect woodpeckers, SERPPAS took a more proactive stance with the gopher tortoise. A fellow species of the longleaf pine habitat, the tortoise is found on many military bases in the Southeast and is considered endangered in some areas. In 2007, SERPPAS developed a partnership to create a conservation agreement to protect the species's habitat. The Gopher Tortoise Candidate Conservation Agreement is voluntary and assists the parties to share and implement best practices for conservation to protect the tortoise (Figure 8-3). This agreement is aimed at helping the gopher tortoise population recover so that it will not need to be listed as threatened or endangered under the Endangered Species Act. It can be used as a model to protect other animals as well.

Another environmental issue that affects health in the Southeast is the impact of climate change on coastal resilience. To the Department of Defense, climate change is understood as a national security threat. Challenges

FIGURE 8-3. SERPPAS partners release gopher tortoises on Eglin Air Force Base as part of a larger conservation strategy for the species. (*Credit*: SERPPAS)

include hurricanes that have damaged bases and flooding and coastal erosion that make maintaining bases more difficult. These impacts affect residential communities, too, including where military personnel and their families live. To enhance coordination of efforts in these defense-supporting communities, SERPPAS partnered with the Georgia Sea Grant Law Program at the University of Georgia. That program, funded by the National Oceanic and Atmospheric Administration, supports university-based programs, including extension programs, that carry out research and education on challenges to coastal areas. SERPPAS and the Sea Grant program—which had not previously partnered with the Department of Defense—hosted a 2019 meeting of a large group of stakeholders to connect the program with military bases and the Southeast state agency partners. This led to several pilot projects. Additionally, SERPPAS developed a partnership with Pew Charitable Trusts to enhance coastal and oyster habitats near military sites.[32]

And following the longleaf restoration initiative's successful approach, in 2021 SERPPAS partnered with Pew to launch a multistakeholder initiative to conserve salt marshes, which span more than a million acres from

North Carolina to Florida. The initiative is called the South Atlantic Salt Marsh Initiative, and its slogan is "Marsh Forward!" Salt marshes protect the coast from floods and other risks, serve as a habitat for fish and other animals, and support many coastal industries. They are threatened by overdevelopment and sea level rise. Protecting them benefits the ecology, environmental health, and economies of both communities and military installations in the Southeast. This work continues as a priority of the SERPPAS Coastal Resilience and Regional Adaptation workgroup, which also supports the goals of the Department of Defense's climate adaptation plan.[33]

Keys to Success

Unconventional partners coming together, and the trust they have built over time, are major contributors to SERPPAS's success. According to Bill Ross, "there is significant power" in bringing together partners that can deliver "a combination of benefits—quality of life, national defense, economic benefit from sustaining these military and economic engines that are so important to the states, as well as communities connected to working farms and forests. All of those things, indirect or direct, deliver an important health benefit. And if you bring unconventional partners together, you have a political power that you don't have operating separately or singly."

Addie Thornton, SERPPAS coordinator, emphasizes the importance of realizing that "you may have partners coming to the table to accomplish completely different missions, but actually they are complementary. We can find those overlaps." She offers another example: The Department of Defense doesn't want a parcel of land developed because they want to fly low over it, the Department of Agriculture because they want it to stay working land, and Fish and Wildlife Service because it is home to an important species. The different interests of the state and federal partners often turn out to be overlapping or compatible.

Jeff Marcus, longleaf pine applied scientist at The Nature Conservancy, echoes the importance of building trust among perhaps strange bedfellows. "Everyone came to the table with good intent and listened to each other," notes an article from the organization. As the woodpecker's recovery shows, "instead of fighting, we can work together to meet the needs of the species and the interests of landowners."[34]

SERPPAS represents "an interesting transition," says Ross. When it began, "everyone was silo-bound, thinking that 'we can take care of our business if we focus on what's happening inside our fence line, our silos,'" he observes. "But there was a growing awareness that you cannot accomplish your mission unless you take action based on what's happening in your external environment."

Both Ross and Thornton underscore the benefits of having these working relationships in place even before an issue arises.

Other areas of the country have taken note. SERPPAS gave rise to the Western Regional Partnership, a similar type of collaboration that includes federal, tribal, and state officials in Arizona, California, Colorado, Nevada, New Mexico, and Utah. The Western Regional Partnership "provides a proactive and collaborative framework" for these officials "to develop solutions that support WRP Partners and protect natural and cultural resources, while promoting sustainability, homeland security and military readiness.[35] SERPPAS's work also contributed to the development of the Sentinel Landscapes Partnership, a broad coalition that includes local governments and is supported at the federal level by the Department of Defense, Department of Agriculture, Department of the Interior, and Federal Emergency Management Agency. It works to advance sustainable land use practices around military installations, and it has expanded nationally. DoD's REPI program, which works with military installations across the US states and territories, has been an important leader in all of these efforts.

For all of these programs, regional characteristics are important. For the Southeastern states that are part of SERPPAS, the partners "share space and they share a landscape. They share resources that extend beyond their state boundaries. That's why SERPPAS exists," says Thornton. It is similar for the Western group. The Sentinel Landscapes effort, she says, is more targeted than SERPPAS, "anchored by one or a few installations in a specific area and building a partnership to that specific geography." This can take place anywhere, depending on how issues are affecting the overlapping missions of agencies. "They ask, 'How can we best leverage our resources toward these overlapping landscape goals?'" A range of projects is possible, such as developing an agreement to protect land abutting a base that development is hindering or addressing an eroding coastline.

❦

RGGI and SERPPAS differ in that the RGGI partnership is composed only of states, while SERPPAS includes the federal government and numerous partners. RGGI brings together states to undertake the same overall goal: to reduce emissions that contribute to climate change. SERPPAS partners started with differing objectives—protect endangered species, maintain buffer zones around military bases to better enable their operations—but found that seeking common solutions was more effective than doing so separately. What might have been a competitive dynamic is instead collaborative.

But RGGI and SERPPAS have much in common. Both accomplish more by working together than each state could accomplish on its own. More partners mean more resources and knowledge to bring to addressing a challenge, greater cost-effectiveness, and broad, long-lasting solutions. And while federal laws, such as the Endangered Species Act, drive some of these actions, the solutions are not top-down regulatory approaches, which were common in the early days of environmental health protection, but tend to spring from local and regional concerns and involve local and regional solutions.

Could such multistate (and beyond) compacts be the wave of the future? A 2018 opinion piece in the *American Journal of Public Health* by Kenneth Olden, a former director of the National Institute of Environmental Health Sciences, addresses this question in the context of the EPA's evolving role. He notes that much pollution today is "scattered," such as farm runoff and emissions that drift across state lines. Therefore, he writes, preventing such problems "will require more collaborative approaches involving the federal government and multiple states." He believes the EPA's role should shift to working with states "in developing clear national goals," developing tools for monitoring progress, and providing financial resources to poorer states to implement environmental health policies. Overall, EPA should "grant more flexibility to state and local governments in achieving their goals."[36]

This sentiment aligns with others who have suggested that Washington should move from regulating to supporting—although in the case of RGGI, there was no federal involvement. Indeed, during the COVID pandemic, two groups of adjacent states—in the Northeast and in the Midwest—joined forces to share personal protective equipment when there were shortages of those important items. A federal–state joint effort, however, might have been ideal.

Both RGGI and SERPPAS boast track records of success spanning twenty years. As discussions and debates over environmental health continue, there is much to learn from their experiences.

NINE

Empowering State Action

Each of the state examples in this book emphasizes a particular policy solution that can lead to improved environmental health protection; many exemplify several policy solutions, which are often cross-cutting and build on each other. For example, increasing environmental health education, emphasized in chapter 4, is foundational to achieving the other policy goals. Collaborating across agencies, the focus of chapter 6, is important in the context of most examples of state success.

This chapter describes the policy goals that public health professionals and others with a stake in stronger state environmental health policies should work toward. Most have been addressed previously in this book, and a few are added here. These policy goals are also relevant to the local and regional levels.

1. Increase environmental health education in university graduate programs—and before

Ironically, at a time of unprecedented challenges in environmental health, Master of Public Health programs are cutting back instruction on this subject. Part of this predicament stems from a 2016 decision by the Council on Education for Public Health (CEPH), the body that accredits public health programs, to remove environmental health sciences as one of five core areas of knowledge required to earn a graduate degree. This change took place as part of a shift to a model that emphasizes "competencies" more than knowledge of core subject areas. Two competencies, for example, are interpreting results of data analysis for use in public health functions and assessing population characteristics that affect communities' health. One learning objective is "explain the effects of environmental factors on a population's health"—but none of the competencies directly addresses environmental health.[1]

Prior to the shift, all students were required to complete coursework in environmental health sciences. As of December 2019, three years after the curriculum changes took effect, just 74 percent of MPH programs required a course in environmental health sciences.[2] According to an analysis by Carly Levy and colleagues in the *American Journal of Public Health*, between 2017 and 2019, environmental health concentrations or degrees were added to nine out of 122 accredited MPH programs but were removed from nineteen. "As a consequence of these significant revisions," the authors write, "public health educational programs are no longer required to graduate a resultant public health workforce competent in [environmental health]."[3]

Many local and state health department staff are already short on environmental health knowledge, and this further lack of training will not help. Additionally, several certifying bodies for public health professionals require environmental health knowledge, and young graduates who take these exams are now less likely to be prepared. These cuts also hurt other professionals-in-training, such as preventive medicine residents, who are required to take an environmental health course to pass their board exam.

Yet students are requesting *more* environmental health content. An unscientific perusal of websites for university public health degree and certificate programs suggests that a new focus on environmental health is emerging. COVID, natural disasters worsened by climate change, and concerns about disparities in health outcomes could all be contributors.

This interest also springs from medical students and residents. A 2023 article in *Stat* describes a push by medical students and recent graduates to include climate change in their training programs.[4] For instance, when Cecilia Sorensen, now an emergency medicine physician, was completing her residency, she saw the health effects of climate change firsthand and wondered why the topic was not addressed in her training. Today, she directs the Global Consortium on Climate and Health Education. Efforts like hers have led to inclusion of climate change in the curricula of several medical schools and in continuing education programs. However, the schools are facing a "bandwidth" challenge, the article explains: Some students want this material embedded throughout their education, but faculty members' understanding of the topic varies.

Additionally, it is unclear whether this expansion extends to environmental health issues beyond climate change, such as toxics in air, water, soil, and consumer products and their impacts on health. Even with the hopeful push among younger students and practitioners to incorporate climate change into training and practice, there is still an acute need to address environmental health broadly. Physicians are increasingly on the front lines of treating patients who have suffered toxic exposures—with the East Palestine train derailment as a dramatic example. And long-term health impacts of chronic, lower-level toxic exposures are treated by physicians daily, often without the needed knowledge.

Mindful of this gap, the Association for Prevention Teaching and Research is working to strengthen public health and medical education by encouraging a focus on disease prevention. The organization develops and provides resources for universities and training programs, and it organized a working group of its members to improve environmental health coursework in the face of CEPH's new lack of an environmental health-specific competency.[5]

This discussion is not only happening within academia. Examples of the need for more environmental health training—both directly related to climate change and not—are also surfacing in the news. A 2024 *New York Times* article detailed a physician's effort to ascertain a diagnosis for her fever, chills, aches, and diarrhea after returning from an island off Venezuela. The practitioners she consulted were perplexed. Then it occurred to her to ask for a test for dengue fever, which turned out to be the culprit. "Despite my training in medicine, I was blindsided," she writes. Noting that the illness was surging south of the United States, likely due to climate change–related weather changes, the writer urges reforms in medical education to prepare for more infectious diseases and other impacts.[6]

Even veterinarians are getting in on the act. While vets and public health experts typically stay in their own silos, growing attention to zoonotic diseases—which are spread between people and animals—has advanced the concept of One Health, the interconnection and interdependence of the health of people, animals, and the environment. Veterinarians who understand that environmental health is part of this paradigm prioritize working toward clean and sustainable air, water, and food to benefit both people and animals.

Breaking through silos is also important when it comes to sharing data on environmental health. This issue arose among participants in a workshop to review the CDC's National Environmental Public Health Tracking Network. The tracking program funds states to strengthen their efforts to collect and track data on environmental threats to public health; currently, thirty-two states and one municipality participate.[7] (Note: This program was significantly cut in the first half of 2025.) Despite successes, the program has been hindered by the fragmentation of the environmental and health fields. The workshop participants noted the need to make more policymakers and stakeholders aware that this program offers useful data that show how environmental conditions affect health outcomes. They recommended broader partnerships between the program and academic groups to better incorporate new scientific information from university research studies into tracking. They also recommended working with the Association of Schools and Programs of Public Health to support training students in how to do this kind of tracking and use its data in research. Training community organizations and health care entities to use it could also build broader support to continue and expand the tracking network.[8]

Local health departments have an important educational role too. Public health education is considered an essential service of LHDs. Leaders should be able to explain how environmentally beneficial activities such as waste reduction and energy efficiency improve health—and save money to boot. For example, a town's residents might wonder why they are being asked to compost food scraps and leave them outside for pickup, when this takes more time and effort than throwing waste in the trash. The health director—via a public service announcement, interview with the local paper, and talks to school and community groups—can explain that trash must be transported hundreds of miles to a landfill, creating diesel air pollution from trucks and soil and air pollution from the landfill. Towns also pay tipping fees to dispose of garbage, which are footed by taxpayers. Composting can reduce air pollution emissions linked to respiratory illness, create rich soil to use in the local community garden, and maybe even reduce fees residents pay. The health director should be able to clearly connect these dots for residents and local organizations. National polls often find that the environment ranks low on voters' list of priorities, and environmental sustainability often gets sidelined as a "luxury" when school or town budgets get tight. But when the local health director explains these connections clearly, making use of data, actions that benefit both the environment and health are more likely to garner broad support.

And while it is critical to prepare professionals to address complex, interdisciplinary environmental health issues and to provide environmental health information to community members, instruction should start earlier and can be incorporated into existing curricula—even for students in elementary school. For example, when children grow tomatoes and spinach in their school gardens, the lessons can encompass the impacts of soil quality and inputs such as fertilizers and pesticides on health.

There is already a program geared to schoolchildren that is available for use by any school, and even by summer camps and before- and after-school programs: EPA's Air Quality Flag Program. Every morning, children check the air quality forecast for that day (available on the EPA's website) and raise the appropriate flag. The different flag colors and their relationship to air quality are depicted in figure 9-1. This program teaches children about the science of air pollution—teachers can plan lessons based on it—and how to protect their own health. It also educates school staff and parents. Figure 9-2 is an activity sheet for kindergarteners provided by the EPA's program.

Environmental health education and awareness are foundational to the successful state case studies in this book. In fact, they are a precondition for development and implementation of strong environmental health policies.

The Air Quality Index	
Index Values	**AQI Category**
0-50	Good (green)
51-100	Moderate (yellow)
101-150	Unhealthy for Sensitive Groups (orange)
151-200	Unhealthy (red)
201-300	Very Unhealthy (purple)
301-500	Hazardous (maroon)

FIGURE 9-1. Air Quality Index. (*Source*: US EPA)

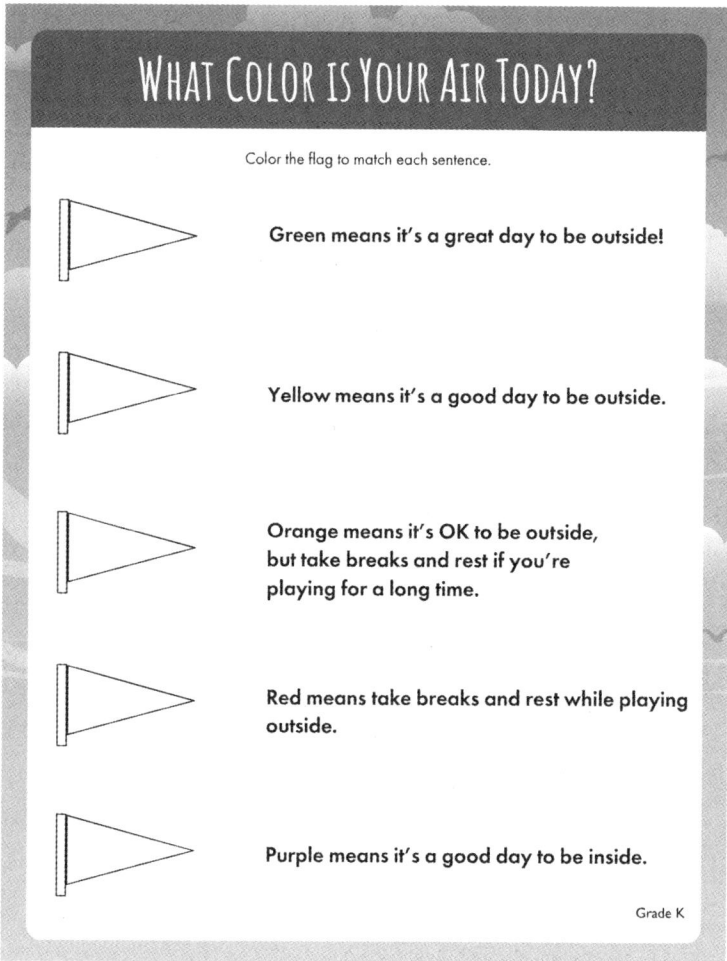

FIGURE 9-2. EPA Air Quality Flag Program activity sheet. (*Source:* US EPA)

2. Carry out expansive economic analyses that account for costs and benefits to families, the health care system, and taxpayers

Prevailing wisdom tells us that the greener, environmentally friendlier option always costs more than its conventional (i.e., dirtier, more toxic) alternative. Polls of voter priorities typically find that support for environmental policies falls when economic concerns rise. But this perception of a zero-sum game is false, because economic analyses often do not account for the full range of impacts. For example, while measures to improve indoor air quality at schools might at first glance appear costly, their economic benefits can be far-reaching—such as improved school attendance and performance, leading to better educational outcomes and higher future earnings. These improvements benefit not only individuals but society as a whole. So it is critical to balance consideration of costs with evaluation of a wide range of benefits.

Economic analyses have been central to the successful implementation of many of the policies described in this book. They were key to New York State's decision to invest in the occupational health and children's environmental health clinic networks. Similarly, the goal of the Massachusetts Toxics Use Reduction Act was to make the state a safer place to live and work while improving its business competitiveness. Analysts have looked at a wide range of economic costs and benefits of TURA, and the data is positive. A 2021 government report found that in reducing the use of toxics, the law lowered worker exposures, toxic releases to the environment, and waste. These benefits have created efficiencies, financial savings, product improvements, and better environmental performance.[9] One simple example is a dry cleaner that switched to nontoxic "wet cleaning." When the Massachusetts Toxics Use Reduction Institute compared the store's before-and-after costs, including for maintenance, detergent, and electricity, it found that the change saved money overall and conserved resources.[10]

Economic analysis has provided support for not only regulations but health interventions. A group of University of Massachusetts Lowell researchers associated with TURI wrote a series of articles making the business case for investing in health programs. They ask: Is this program a good investment? Will it provide benefits and save money? One analysis looked at the cost benefits of "in-home environmental interventions" to help people manage asthma—nurses or social workers visiting individual homes to identify possible asthma triggers and providing items such as HEPA filters or mattress covers.[11] The benefits included fewer trips to the emergency room and fewer workdays lost—both of which have a clear monetary benefit. Such studies have been used to make the case for Medicaid and other health insurance programs to cover asthma home visits.

The savings outlined in these analyses can be expansive. For example, a study by health policy researcher Elise Gould found that controlling household lead paint to reduce blood lead levels in a cohort of at-risk children had a tremendous economic payoff: Every dollar invested in lead paint hazard control yielded a return of between $17 and $221.[12] The benefits quantified include reduction in health care costs, in special education services needed, and in IQ loss leading to lower lifetime earnings and associated potential loss of tax revenue for the government, among others. Expansive indeed— and Gould notes that her estimates of the benefits of lead hazard control are conservative.

Highlighting cost savings and efficiencies can make environmental health policies more appealing to a broad range of policymakers of different political persuasions. Participants in a workshop to review the CDC's National Environmental Public Health Tracking Network noted, "Reframing tracking stories to analyze the return on investment for more strategic allocation of resources" helps to demonstrate the network's value. They give the example of tracking data that demonstrated average cancer rates in a community and thus avoided a disease cluster investigation "that would likely have been very costly and taken years to complete."

3. Expand government-university-industry partnerships

Partnerships are a cornerstone of TURA and of Texas's school Integrated Pest Management law. Universities' roles in these partnerships can support policy solutions by providing environmental health education, technical assistance, and broad economic analyses of programs. Some advocates recommend that universities take on these roles, since government agencies may not possess necessary expertise in-house and studies from academia are likely to be freer from political pressure. This may be especially the case given generally declining research resources in state government.

And industry should be part of the solution—not in terms of industry-funded research, which raises serious conflict-of-interest concerns—but as partners in developing innovations and solutions that improve environmental health. Industry partners often have the on-the-ground knowledge about how things work, like the dry cleaners who had the day-to-day experience of using two different machines, processes, and products—and observed the impacts firsthand. In the Texas school IPM program, pesticide applicators are primary partners because they are called in to treat pest problems. To comply with the law, they must have the appropriate training and tools. When universities and government agencies do not already have working relationships, they should develop them—and industry should be brought in as collaborators. Many resources to bring these groups together should already be in place, especially since many state universities already have active extension programs.

Such partnerships are also the focus of recommendations for strengthening the CDC's national Environmental Public Health Tracking Program. Growing tracking infrastructure and incorporating emerging scientific approaches like biomonitoring and epigenetics in the tracking program require building broader partnerships with academic entities.[13] There is also potential to link environmental health tracking data with health care organizations to support them in developing community health needs assessments.

4. Take local action

When a local government develops and implements an innovative program or policy, and evaluates its impacts, costs, benefits, community reactions, and lessons learned, that information can be persuasive when approaching state legislators to ask for a statewide policy.

There are many examples. School IPM working groups have organized pilot events in which they bring together school staff, pest control professionals, university extension educators, and government staff to learn how to establish IPM in schools. The goal: for participants to support IPM in schools as the norm across states.[14] Community health centers, hospitals, and local organizations have worked to provide transportation to health care appointments for patients who lack a car, a ride, or funds to pay for a cab. These efforts to reduce transportation barriers save money since the residents are more likely to have their health care needs met and avoid visits to the emergency room. In Vermont, for example, two communities had developed such programs, and the outcomes were promising. They were then selected as pilot areas in a statewide "Rides to Wellness" project that aimed to expand such efforts across Vermont.[15]

On a more local level, the city of Takoma Park, Maryland, enacted an ordinance restricting the use of pesticides for cosmetic purposes on both public and private property. (Maryland does not have a state preemption law.) After its enactment, advocates aimed to achieve the same policy in

Montgomery County, in which Takoma Park is located. Although several lawsuits were filed opposing it, this effort was ultimately successful. While the policy never reached the state level, it is an example of a smaller unit of government influencing a larger one.

Numerous networks and organizations can provide information and assistance with developing and carrying out local efforts. These include ICLEI-Local Governments for Sustainability, Urban Sustainability Directors Network, International City/County Management Association, Institute for Sustainable Communities, and Big Cities Health Coalition.

5. End state preemption of local policymaking

State preemption of local policymaking has increased in recent years and become a widespread concern among public health professionals. Preemption has prevented local governments from acting on issues such as menu labeling, gun restrictions, hydraulic fracturing (fracking), and inclusionary zoning policies that aim to increase development of affordable housing.

In the pesticide arena, a city that wishes to limit use of more hazardous pesticides on residential or business property will run straight into the preemption barrier if it is in one of the forty-plus states with such a law, which preempts local authority to restrict pesticide use. There is variation between states, with some having explicit preemption while others require proponents of a local action to petition a state commission or board to take an action they desire. In some towns, for instance, environmental advocates concerned about protecting pollinators and wildlife want to ban neonicotinoid insecticides, which are extremely toxic to bees in particular. But if they live in a preemption state, they must convince the state to take action, which can be challenging.

Yet even in states with preemption laws, both state and local governments have been able to make a meaningful difference through policies that reduce pesticide use on public property and by providing education, information, and technical assistance. These are major components of the school IPM program in Texas, which has a preemption law but a state government that actively addresses this area, requiring that all schools statewide implement IPM practices. (If a municipality wished to go further than state laws, they could encounter restrictions.) On the local level, San Francisco's pest management policy is considered one of the best in the country, and its resources for its city departments are looked to nationally as best practices.[16] A growing number of city and county governments are developing and implementing policies to reduce not only pesticide use but also synthetic fertilizer use, which can contribute to algae growth in waterways.

So what is behind the broader preemption trend, and how can local governments recover their independence? The National League of Cities identifies some of the contributors to the "worsening hostility" between statehouses and local governments.[17] Corporate lobbying and influence aim to economically benefit the regulated industries (a clear factor in my own largely agricultural state's preemption of local pesticide restrictions). A major player in this effort, the business group American Legislative Exchange Council, writes preemption bills that can be handed directly to friendly legislators. Another factor is when there is a political mismatch between the interests of a state and of its largest city—the so-called blue city, red state conflict—which may be exacerbated by an increase in local governments moving forward with developing new and innovative policies.

According to the National League of Cities, reversing the trend of preemption will require a range of actions by local leaders, including educating the public about the impacts of preemption, pulling together broad coalitions to advocate to protect local democracy, and challenging preemption laws in court. The organization's action guide provides numerous examples.

Additionally, the CDC identifies several methods local governments have used to overcome state preemption in enacting public health policies. These include identifying a purpose for a local law that is different from the purpose of the state law. For example, a Los Angeles ordinance required retailers to post signs warning that alcohol consumption during pregnancy could cause birth defects. The city framed it as a health warning to avoid being preempted by a state law prohibiting certain kinds of advertising on signs.[18] Another route local governments can take is asserting home rule rights. CDC notes that Cleveland, Ohio's city council successfully defended its ban on trans fats by arguing that a state law limiting local governments' ability to regulate restaurants infringed on its home rule rights, under which states grant localities some autonomy.[19] Finally, local laws may be safer from preemption challenges if they closely track the language of the law at the higher level of government.

6. Increase collaboration of agencies that impact environmental health

If a school pesticide policy is implemented by a state agriculture department, its staff may not have the requisite background to include health impacts in the information it provides. But if the agriculture agency partners with the state environmental and public health agencies, together they can provide much more information about the policy's environmental and occupational health rationale, costs, and benefits. The Health in All Policies model, as in the Tennessee and Colorado examples in chapter 6, is a way of achieving this kind of collaboration. So are health impact assessments (HIAs), which bring together a range of agencies and other partners to evaluate how a proposed plan, program, or policy is likely to affect a community's health. While HIAs are for the most part neither required nor carried out routinely, they are becoming more common.

Johns Hopkins's Thomas Burke notes that states' capacities to evaluate environmental health risks has not kept pace with the demand. Progress, he writes, will require "improved cooperation between the many health and environmental agencies in the complex 'environmental web' to assure that they do not lose sight of their fundamental mission—the protection of public health."[20]

Government agency collaborations to address environmental health can naturally extend to the health care sector, especially in the context of the community health needs assessments that nonprofit hospitals are required to develop under the Affordable Care Act. When hospitals assess the health needs of the communities they serve, and develop strategies to meet those needs, two-way sharing of data and innovations with state and local health departments that often carry out similar evaluations can benefit all institutions involved and reduce duplication of effort. And as a growing number of hospitals are undertaking efforts to address social determinants of health—such as by building affordable housing and greening their own facilities and operations to reduce pollution that contributes to the illnesses they treat—opportunities for collaboration can be multifaceted. As just one example, Cleveland Clinic and two other nearby health systems have worked with the regional transportation agency to support expansions like a new bus rapid transit route. Such a collaboration might seem unexpected, but benefits cited include reducing air pollution while helping patients get to medical appointments.

And given the hugely varied contributors to and impacts of climate change, it will be difficult to address this broad problem if environmental health is treated separately from areas such as food, housing, transportation, and energy.

7. Expand policy surveillance and legal epidemiology research

Researchers and practitioners working at the intersection of law and public health have pointed out that public health data, like asthma and cancer diagnoses and blood lead levels, are routinely gathered and made use of at many levels of government. Yet laws and policies that can have major impacts on these health outcomes are not considered. As Scott Burris of the Center for Public Health Law Research at Temple University's law school puts it, we take for granted that health information can be collected electronically and merged with demographic and other information to further our understanding of population health conditions. But information about public health laws, their implementation, and their impacts on health largely "remains trapped in text files and pdfs . . . excluded from the universe of usable data."[21] Policies that address health are not routinely identified or tracked. Government agencies implement health laws but may not assess whether they are working as intended.

To address these shortcomings, Burris and others highlight the importance of policy surveillance, defined as "the ongoing systematic, scientific collection and analysis of laws of public health significance."[22] This typically involves mapping public health laws across states, cities, or institutions. Sometimes lawyers carry out this work, but not always. One example of an organization that does this kind of mapping is the Guttmacher Institute. It tracks laws relating to abortion, which encompasses a huge array of topics: advertising restrictions, bans, provider qualifications, requirements for minors, waiting period requirements, insurance coverage restrictions, facility licensing requirements, and more. The organization's database is needed because the laws, which vary enormously from state to state, are complicated and confusing, constantly changing, and regularly challenged in court. This makes it difficult for practitioners and advocates to keep up with changes or understand the laws' impacts.[23] The National League of Cities also carries out policy surveillance. It tracks state preemption of various kinds of policies to help cities prepare for preemption limitations, encourage research about reasons for preemption and its impacts, and ensure transparency.[24]

When policy surveillance is carried out routinely and its findings made easily accessible, it is endlessly useful to governments working on a particular public health problem. They can use this data to find out how others are addressing the issue, and it encourages "diffusion of innovation" as one sector of government learns about solutions from others.[25]

Going another step forward, policy surveillance is a component of legal epidemiology, which is "the scientific study of law as a factor in the cause, distribution and prevention of disease in a population."[26] This goes to a second kind of evaluation: using scientific research methods to study the impact of laws on actual public health outcomes, using regulations as data, and bridging the legal and public health disciplines. Laws addressing areas as varied as immigration, car safety, tobacco, unemployment compensation, and drug prescribing can have major public health impacts. Understanding these impacts can lead to broader enactment of laws that improve health and reconsideration of those that are less effective.

Legal epidemiology is a new field, and there is much to do. The CDC has identified legal epidemiology competencies, and there is great potential for this area to grow within academic and practice realms.[27] Public health policy data sets and tools can be used to develop so-called 50 State Surveys (compilations of laws across the states addressing a particular topic) and health law profiles of specific states, and can be useful in expanding Health in All Policies efforts.[28]

Doug Farquhar, a lawyer and the government affairs director at the National Environmental Health Association, emphasizes the need for increased funding and training for legal epidemiology studies in order to understand which environmental health policies have the greatest impact on public health. He also stresses the need for national metrics as a precondition for this work. He believes the federal government is best suited to collect data and develop national metrics—and provide it to the states to jump-start their own research. He notes that the large, federal National Health and Nutrition Examination Survey (NHANES), which assesses the health and nutritional status of Americans, provides a useful national snapshot. "We need [an NHANES equivalent] state by state," he says. "What are people in Mississippi or Minnesota dying from? What policies contribute to that?" Again, understanding what policies are effective in a certain state, and why, can be instructive to other states as they consider environmental health policies. He believes that ranking states on public health metrics can add to the incentive to carry out these studies, since state officials want theirs to be rated as healthy.

8. Re-fund decimated state public health agencies

While public health had a moment in the sun during the COVID pandemic, the overall trend is a decline in funding. Spending on health care is rising—the American Medical Association reports that it grew by 4.1 percent in 2022—and public health spending has fallen.[29] According to the Trust for America's Health, a nonprofit, nonpartisan public health think tank, the CDC's budget for fiscal year 2024 was 3 percent less than its 2023 budget when accounting for inflation, and its budget has increased only 4 percent in the past decade when accounting for inflation.[30] The Trust states that rising rates of chronic disease in the United States are partly due to "decades of underinvestment in public health infrastructure" and in the public health workforce, leaving the country unprepared to meet emerging public health challenges.[31] Public health is more underfunded, relatively speaking, than many other types of government agency programs. Ironically, when public health is doing its job— restaurant kitchens have been inspected and are free of vermin, walking and biking paths provide convenient exercise opportunities—it is invisible and therefore vulnerable to budget cuts.

Public health funding shortfalls at the federal level have a major impact on state public health departments, which are the primary spenders on public health and typically receive most of their revenue from federal sources. Thus, state spending on public health has also decreased, notwithstanding the federal infusion of cash to states to address COVID, which has ended. State cuts to public health programs during the 2007–2009 recession have not been reversed as of this writing. And as always, public health spending takes place in boom or bust cycles, as panic over the latest crisis dies down and defaults to neglect. During the 2024 budget cycle, even large, well-off states like California and Washington discussed cutting public health program funding and laying off staff.

Paul J. Fleming of the University of Michigan School of Public Health and his colleagues offer recommendations for addressing the field's chronic funding problem by shifting to proactively supporting the basic drivers of health. These include changing the focus of public health agencies like the

CDC and the National Institutes of Health from specific diseases and categorization of health issues as either chronic or infectious to, instead, "key foundational drivers of health and well-being." This shift would reflect the understanding that social determinants of health, including environmental conditions, affect population health outcomes, apart from concern about a specific illness. They recommend a broad Health in All Policies approach in which public health professionals regularly collaborate with their colleagues at agencies that address housing, education, public safety, and other drivers of health, and more advocacy by public health professionals in the form of building coalitions and publishing op-eds and fact sheets.[32]

The Trust takes a similar tack, proposing in an article titled "What If Congress Adequately Funded Public Health?" that the country invest in prevention rather than "spending trillions of dollars to treat preventable chronic conditions." The organization argues that if this was done, workers "would be healthier and more productive, employers would face fewer financial burdens, and the nation would be more resilient and thriving." It also notes that Congress rescinded hundreds of millions of dollars that were

TABLE 9-1. How policy solutions underpin and bolster state case study programs and policies

Policy solution	Massachusetts Toxics Use Reduction Act	Texas school Integrated Pest Management law	New York State occupational health and children's environmental health clinic networks
1. Increase environmental health education	Key to TURA's enactment was a knowledgeable group of advocates and academics. TURA encompasses environmental health education that contributes to toxics use reduction.	Environmental health education includes outreach and technical assistance to key IPM personnel and information and updates to school staff and community.	Environmental health awareness was foundational to establishment of the clinics, while the clinics' provision of education and training supports advocacy and expertise for communities.
2. Carry out more expansive economic analyses	A goal is to help make businesses in the state more competitive. TURI carries out expansive cost-benefit analyses, which identify a range of economic benefits for the companies making these changes.	Economic analyses of the program identify cost savings. The IPM Cost Calculator helps to illuminate the link between investments and outcomes.	This was critical in making the case for establishing the clinics and centers.

meant to strengthen the public health workforce and emergency preparedness and response efforts, even after COVID clearly illustrated the country's lack of public health preparation. The Trust recommends a long-term commitment to "stable, predictable public health funding at all levels of government." This includes continued support for the Prevention and Public Health Fund, which was created as part of the Affordable Care Act to promote health and prevent illness and is chronically at risk from budget cutting proposals.[33]

To return to the point that started this chapter, expanding environmental health education can also help to meet this challenge, since it would increase the number of people who are aware of the importance of state and local environmental health policies and programs. They would then be more likely to support stable funding to overcome the cycle of panic and neglect that often leaves public health by the wayside.

Table 9-1 summarizes how policy solutions underpin and bolster state case study programs and policies.

California AB 617 and cumulative impacts	*Tennessee Livability Collaborative and Colorado Health in All Policies Program*	*COVID-19 mitigation in schools*	*Cooperation across states: Regional Greenhouse Gas Initiative and Southeast Regional Partnership for Planning and Sustainability*
Providing environmental health education to steering committee members is a central aspect of their partnerships with Air Districts.	Through collaboration, the health departments' sister agency staff learn about environmental health and include environmental health improvements in program goals.	More and better information about healthy indoor air quality in schools could have improved COVID-19 mitigation, along with better preparing schools for climate change impacts.	Well-informed agency staff who had previously worked with neighboring states to reduce other air pollutants were key to RGGI's successful development. Agency staff's understanding of the impact of Southeast growth patterns on environmental health paved the way for SERPPAS.
Economic disparities, in addition to environmental disparities, are a focus of the law.	Goals include coordinating and leveraging funding, which increases efficiency.	A comprehensive balancing of costs and benefits of possible mitigation actions would have led to more effective decision-making.	RGGI analyses predicted that sales of allowances would benefit states economically and ongoing economic evaluations have quantified these benefits. Originators of SERPPAS understood that the costs of the program would be outweighed by its benefits.

TABLE 9-1. (continued)

Policy solution	Massachusetts Toxics Use Reduction Act	Texas school Integrated Pest Management law	New York State occupational health and children's environmental health clinic networks
3. Expand state agency-university-industry partnerships	State agencies, an institute based at a university, and industry collaborate closely to reduce use of toxics.	The program is based on a partnership encompassing the state legislature and agencies, state university Extension program, school districts, state associations of school boards and school administrators, and the pest control industry.	Clinics align with the state prevention agenda, are funded from a tax on workers' compensation insurance premiums, and work with industry to increase safety and health.
4. Take local action	Local action was one ingredient in achieving state action.	Local/school district education and activities are central components.	Documenting local problems around the state was key to establishing a statewide network.
5. End state preemption of local policymaking		Texas's preemption law for pesticides does not interfere with its school IPM program. But in many states, localities that want to restrict pesticides on private property will run into this roadblock.	
6. Increase collaboration of agencies that impact environmental health	The governing Administrative Council includes representatives of five state agencies: environmental protection, housing and economic development, public health, labor and workforce development, and public safety.	This multidisciplinary, collaborative approach includes the state agriculture department, state boards, and state university Extension.	The centers connect environmental and occupational health, labor, and medicine.
7. Fund and strengthen legal epidemiology to study health impacts of state policies	In general, would help to better understand impacts of these policies and thus speed up that are beneficial while avoiding those found not beneficial.		
8. Re-fund decimated state and local public health agencies.	Sufficient funding is critical for implementation of all of these policy areas.		

(*Source:* Author)

California AB 617 and cumulative impacts	Tennessee Livability Collaborative and Colorado Health in All Policies Program	COVID-19 mitigation in schools	Cooperation across states: Regional Greenhouse Gas Initiative and Southeast Regional Partnership for Planning and Sustainability
Universities have worked with the state on many aspects of the law. Industry is increasingly a partner at the table and discussant on air quality and climate issues.	Partnerships with universities add expertise and reduce duplication.	Broader partnerships— for example, with university healthy buildings experts— would have been helpful.	The broad size and scope of the state partnerships enabled RGGI to draw on the resources of academic researchers, think tanks, and more. The flexibility of the program allowed new businesses to enter the market. SERPPAS includes partners from all three sectors.
Local models helped contribute to a statewide vision.	Local community design models intersect with the state program.	Local agencies play an important role, but they need federal guidance.	Local and regional issues served as the springboard for development and continue to drive actions and solutions.
The more a range of agencies become involved— such as those addressing land use and transportation— the more protective the potential outcomes.	Collaboration of state agencies—currently 20-plus—is the purpose of Tennessee's program. Colorado has developed numerous cross-agency collaborative structures.	While CDC responded, partnerships with agencies like EPA and OSHA could have improved outcomes.	Agency staff working across departments like environment and energy was essential to RGGI's successful development. SERPPAS state agencies include agriculture, environment, fish and wildlife, resilience, and more. Federal agencies also represent a breadth of issues and interests.
the spread of those	In general, legal epidemiology may advance cross-disciplinary work with its findings about effective policies.	In general, would help to better understand impacts of these policies and thus speed up the spread of those that are beneficial while avoiding those found not beneficial.	

TEN

Advocating for Environmental Health Policy

In previous chapters, we explored how smart environmental policy can make a real difference in public health. But how can we ensure that these types of laws and regulations are passed and enforced? Successful advocates agree on several key strategies for keeping pressure on government decision-makers to protect their constituents from harmful exposures and support their well-being.

When a community faces an environmental threat, the first step is to see if a relevant policy already exists to address the problem. If so, it may still take considerable effort to navigate the established system, but at least there is a clear path. If a policy is *not* already on the books, advocacy can make it a reality—a longer road, but one that can lead to critical protections for the community and generations to come. When trying to enact a new law or regulation, it is imperative to build a coalition, identify a champion who is situated to lead on the issue, and garner widespread attention for it by contacting local media, writing opinion pieces, posting on social media, and speaking up at public meetings.

This chapter examines these steps in greater detail, drawing on examples from successful campaigns. Throughout, I will highlight the story of a kindergarten class in New York City that pressured their city council to ban pesticides in city parks and playgrounds by using these strategies. By the time the ban was passed, the kids were in seventh grade. But that is no surprise; this was a big issue and required a big tent to achieve the goal. The timeline and particular challenges will be unique to each advocacy effort, but the contours of winning campaigns share much in common.

RESEARCHING POLICIES

In the case of New York City's parks and playgrounds, a policy was not in place to prohibit pesticide use. But the kids and their adult supporters would not have known this without some basic research. This process can start with a simple call to the local public health or environmental agency, since staff are familiar with the local context and any relevant policies.[1] Ask what they know about the problem, whether there is a policy addressing it, and, if so, who enforces the policy. Local advocacy organizations may also know the answers to these questions and often have staff who are happy to share information with residents. Perusing a locality's ordinances or a state's laws and regulations online can garner additional findings about the potential existence of a policy. A quick online search may turn up news articles about the issue; perhaps others have raised concerns about it or policies addressing it have been discussed.

Another initial step may be filing a complaint. Local health departments must respond to odor complaints, which includes pollution that can be smelled. Filing a complaint can get the ball rolling. This can typically be done on both the local and state levels; information about how to do so, and sometimes an online form, should be provided on the agency's website. Of course, one can directly contact the source of the pollution emission, as perhaps the issue can be resolved informally with expression of concern and provision of information about alternatives. Similarly, one could discuss their concerns with the appropriate staff person at the local health or environmental agency, or with a local or state elected official like a city councilor or state representative.

Beyond understanding environmental health policies in your area, you can get data on pollution and other health threats from public sources such as the EPA's AirNow website, which reports air pollution levels around the country; the EPA's Toxics Release Inventory, which reports pollution emissions to air, water, and soil; the American Lung Association's annual *State of the Air* report; and state maps of properties that are contaminated, usually due to past industrial operations. *Investigating Environmental Contamination: A Guide for Communities*, published by the Region 5 Pediatric Environmental Health Specialty Unit (PEHSU) at the University of Illinois Chicago School of Public Health, details local, state, and federal sources of information about pollution in communities. It describes health conditions that are related to pollution and sources of local data on conditions like asthma, cancer, and birth defects.[2] While comprehensive guides like this that address environmental emissions, related children's health conditions, and advocacy recommendations are not routinely available in other communities, some states provide helpful children's environmental health information. For example, the Vermont Department of Health website includes an "Environmental Health Guide for Parents, Caregivers and Child Care Providers."[3] New Hampshire's Department of Health and Human Services has an interactive online guide to children's environmental health resources that provides information specific to the reader's situation and concerns (e.g., owns or rents, does or does not have children with asthma or allergies).[4] Along with specific data for a particular community, you can seek background information on environmental health issues from local, state, and federal agencies; organizations; news sites; and scientific journals.

When a public record is not available, you can submit a Freedom of Information Act (FOIA) request. With a few exceptions, a publicly funded agency—whether local, state, or federal—must provide it. The Black Institute in New York City used these requests to find out where pesticides had been applied in the city, then used the data to map the locations, thereby making the invisible visible. Since pollution is often hard to see and pinpoint, yet can spread widely through the ecosystem, this was an innovative and persuasive approach.

Policy statements published by professional associations such as the American Public Health Association, American Academy of Pediatrics, and American College of Obstetricians and Gynecologists can be particularly useful since they are written without jargon for a lay audience. For example, the American Academy of Pediatrics published a policy statement, "Pesticide Exposure in Children," that is clear, comprehensive, and includes recommendations addressed to pediatricians and to government decision-makers.[5] The organization's website also has a page on pesticide exposure with straightforward advice about health effects and prevention.[6]

These statements become invaluable if you find that protections are not in place and you need to propose a new policy. Research from professional associations can not only arm you with data but offer examples of important elements to include in any policy solution. National organizations that track proposed and enacted policies can also demonstrate how common a certain type of policy is and provide examples of policies in place around the country. Such organizations include the National Conference of State Legislatures, National Caucus of Environmental Legislators, and Environmental Council of the States. Some agencies provide sample policies, such as the EPA's model IPM policy for schools.

When crafting your own solution, it is imperative to address both costs and benefits. Skeptical policymakers often assume that choosing healthier products or processes will be more expensive. Yet over time, benefits can outweigh costs, and safer products and services can typically be purchased at a discount—for example, through purchasing consortiums or cooperatives. Convincing the powers that be that your solution will not put a strain on public coffers is often key to progress.

When addressing environmental health challenges related to climate change on the state level, policy solutions need to be acceptable across a broad political spectrum. It can help to focus on economic benefits of environmentally sustainable projects and policies. This is especially important in communities where fossil fuels contribute to jobs and the economy. Local projects geared to goals like reducing building energy use, expanding public and active transportation, reducing waste, and developing job training programs to support such programs can provide data on impacts, costs, and benefits that can be marshaled in seeking broader support at the state level.

Sometimes the aim of advocacy is not development of a new policy but enforcement of an existing one. For example, many cities and states have anti-idling laws that limit the amount of time that diesel-fueled buses and trucks can run their engines while parked. Diesel exhaust contains soot particles linked with cancer and heart disease. A *Chicago Tribune* article found that a year after Chicago passed an ordinance limiting idling to three minutes, the police had not written any tickets for violations.[7] When I observed a school bus idling in front of my children's school for a long period of time, I called the bus company and reminded them of the policy. While I don't know whether that call made a difference—I wasn't routinely at the school—

my next step would have been to contact a local official with authority to enforce that law.

BUILDING A COALITION

Building a coalition is a cornerstone of policy advocacy for a reason: While one or two people can be easily dismissed as outliers, a group is harder to ignore. And groups of groups are even more powerful. There is strength in numbers, plus coalitions provide a structure for pooling expertise and uniting groups with overlapping interests. First, look for existing organizations that could serve as a launchpad for advocating on your issue rather than feeling like you have to create a group from scratch. As a personal example, when I was advocating for pesticide reduction to protect my children's health and was struggling to move forward solo, I read about a local environmental organization that was advocating for pesticide reduction to protect pollinators such as bees. I reached out and talked to their point person, who became my ally in all of my efforts from that point on. Although her focus differed from mine, pesticide reduction would help both of us achieve our goals. Whereas I had a strong science background, she understood how to carry out outreach to the public and the media. Our combined skills made our effort stronger.

Research groups and coalitions that could be good places for making such contacts. A few examples: North Shore Green Women connects environmental health advocates from numerous Chicago suburbs. The Safer Chemicals, Healthy Families coalition includes dozens of state and national environmental and health organizations that joined together to call for reform of the outdated Toxics Substances Control Act.[8] Californians for Pesticide Reform is a coalition of more than 170 organizations dedicated to this goal. An online search will turn up local and state groups that may address concerns like yours.

Jen Walling, executive director of the Illinois Environmental Council, gives examples of broad allyship leading to success. Her organization teamed up with pharmacies to support a bill addressing safe disposal of prescription drugs, and that partnership moved the legislation forward. When advocating for more bottle-refill stations to reduce plastic waste, she developed an effective coalition with both plumbers and public health groups.

Similarly, climate change policies have been more successful with coalitions that include the renewable energy industry, real estate and insurance companies, and manufacturers of heating, ventilation, and air-conditioning systems.[9] Meanwhile, a report by the Network for Public Health Law observes that numerous potential public health allies at the local and state levels remain "untapped resources."[10] These include state associations of city and county health officials, American Public Health Association and Public Health Institute state affiliates, the American Heart Association and American Lung Association and their state or local affiliates, groups advocating for healthier housing and transportation, rural health associations, university research and policy centers, and environmental and environmental justice groups. It also suggests creating a public health caucus or commission within a state legislature, citing Indiana and Maryland as examples.

The idea of creating a new legislative caucus or bringing together vast constituencies can seem daunting, so it is worth remembering that the seeds of coalitions can be quite small and found in unexpected places. Take, for instance, our classroom of New York kindergarteners. The children's concern was piqued in 2014 when their teacher, Paula Rogovin, as part of researching food in their school cafeteria, taught them about how synthetic pesticides can harm people, the environment, and pets. Rather than leaving the students feeling helpless about the problem, she led them in coming up with a solution. When the local city councilor, Ben Kallos, visited the school, the children explained that they were angry about the use of pesticides and that they had talked about ways to make change. The class came up with a demand: "Ban toxic pesticides. Use only nature's pesticides. Pass a law!" They wrote a play and performed it for parents and the rest of the school to educate them about the issue.[11]

Kallos invited the class to visit city hall and asked how he could help. Shortly after, the World Health Organization declared glyphosate, the main ingredient in the herbicide Roundup, a possible carcinogen. Based on that information, Kallos in 2015 introduced the bill that the kindergarteners wanted. It would have banned city agencies from applying synthetic pesticides in parks. The bill was "laid over," or put off. For a couple of years, there was no progress. Then, in 2017, a hearing was scheduled by the council's health committee. Dozens of children from the school attended and performed a play. "They let us in with all our signs because these were little kids," says Rogovin. "The media was there. . . . The kids were interviewed, parents, grandparents were interviewed."[12]

But given the lengthy nature of the political process, the bill still did not get passed. So the school group spent the following year "working with the environmental groups from all over the city" to improve the bill, Rogovin explains, and it was reintroduced.[13] While the original bill banned substances included on an EPA list, the 2019 bill went further, additionally banning substances classified as toxic by California's Office of Environmental Health Hazard Assessment.[14]

Following the bill's 2019 reintroduction, it was again referred to committee, laid over, approved by committee, amended by committee, and so forth. As time went on, and the children and their families kept up the pressure, they were joined by "an expanding circle of grown-up allies," according to *The New York Times*.[15] A forum held at the school included researchers who examine pesticide issues, as well as staff of the nonprofit organization Beyond Pesticides. City and parks staff harbored doubts about the proposed changes—not surprising, since they would require a different way of doing things and a learning curve that would require extra time at first. "But as word of the bill spread," *The New York Times* reported, "public-housing residents and environmental groups teamed up with Ms. Rogovin's students and their parents in a widening circle."

The coalition included physicians and other experts from the Department of Environmental Medicine & Public Health of Mount Sinai's Icahn School of Medicine.[16] The Black Institute, the research and advocacy organization mentioned earlier, also supported the bill. They used public data, supplemented with public information requests, to learn where pesticides were applied in New York City and found that areas with largely Black and Latino populations were disproportionately sprayed. Black and Latino parks employees were also more likely to have contact with glyphosate. These findings, and the group's report *Poison Parks*, brought more concerned families into the coalition.[17]

When the reintroduced bill finally reached the city council—with the added prohibition of pesticide active ingredients listed by the International Agency for Research on Cancer—the vote to pass it into law was unanimous.[18] By banning use of synthetic pesticides in city parks and playgrounds—with limited exceptions for emergency situations—the law was meant to move agencies to use of "biological" or natural pesticides.

While the champion for this effort, Councilor Kallos, emerged early in the process, the proposed ban did not progress until a broad range of stakeholders came on board. This process was supported by education—such as the play the kindergarteners performed to provide information about the cause—and regularly and persistently getting the issue into the local news media. For example, on the day Kallos introduced the revised bill in 2019, a press release included supporting statements from the Natural Resources Defense Council, Grassroots Environmental Education, and Beyond Pesticides.[19]

Following the bill's passage in 2021, a coalition formed to ensure implementation of the new law. Implementation often requires at least as much advocacy as getting a policy passed, which is just the first step. The group, which called itself the Eco-Friendly Parks for All coalition, asked the city's parks department to set up demonstration sites to show how nonchemical lawn care works. The group asked for quick action so that the city would be prepared to implement the policy at its start date and obtained a donation from Stonyfield Organic to cover needed consulting services to manage the sites. In addition to the organizations listed above, the coalition counts among its members The Black Institute, Children's Environmental Health Center at the Icahn School of Medicine at Mount Sinai, and Voters for Animal Rights.[20]

IDENTIFYING A CHAMPION

Councilor Kallos was an ideal champion: He was perfectly situated to make a change by introducing and pressing for passage of a bill. He was positioned to communicate with and influence fellow city councilors and other decision-makers. Fortunately for this effort, Kallos seemed to grasp the significance of the issue right away. He wrote, "All families should be able to enjoy our city parks without having to worry that they are being exposed to toxic pesticides that could give them and their families cancer." He noted that, as a new parent, he did not allow his daughter to play on the grass since a baby puts things in their mouth, and that could include toxins in the park. "I look forward to working with all of our city agencies to ban toxic pesticides and keep our children safe," Kallos wrote.[21]

While Kallos was particularly effective, strong champions can be found in many different quarters. In Vermont, school nurses recognized the health risks of air fresheners and helped to get them out of school buildings by reaching out to the state health department for assistance and support. In Illinois, supporters of banning neonicotinoid pesticides met with their state representative who had a strong track record on environmental issues and understood the dynamics of the political system. The advocates for funding of the New York State clinics approached state legislators from both parties who chaired health and environment committees, understood the importance of the proposal, and were in a position to build support.

To identify the people or organizations that are most critical to your advocacy efforts, the Region 5 PEHSU handbook recommends an exercise called "power mapping." This visual tool encompasses five steps:

1. Determine your target—the person you need to influence so they can solve the problem.
2. Map the influences on your target, such as donors and organizations that support or work with them. For example, if a school facilities manager has the power to make the change you seek, include the voters who elect the school board, which appoints the school superintendent, who hires the operations chief, who supervises the facilities manager who is your target. Students, youth soccer groups, and anyone else with a stake or interest in the school's facilities could also be included. The guide suggests taking a broad view and creating a visual "web of connections."
3. Determine how groups or people within a network influence each other and note any that connect to you or your group.
4. Identify the highest-priority groups among those you have identified.
5. Use the power map to develop advocacy strategies.[22]

Figure 10-1 is an example of a power map. It depicts connections to Lisa Jones, a fictional state representative whom the advocate wants to persuade to propose a law that would reduce emissions from a local hazardous waste site. These include a running club that Rep. Jones participates in, the members of which might be affected by the emissions—and same for the church she attends, which counts among its members several runners as well as others who live near the site. The high school and university may have on-staff experts on pollution who could inform Rep. Jones and other policymakers about the risk of the emissions.

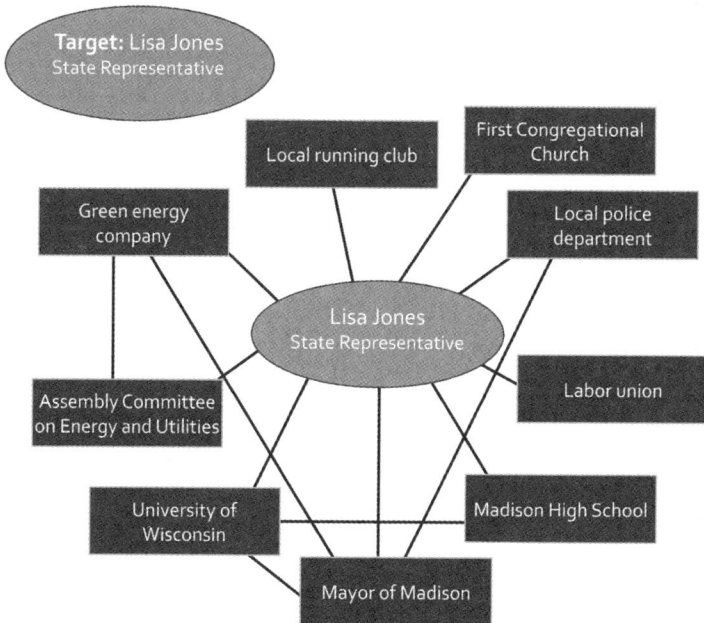

Figure 10-1. Example of power map for identifying targets of advocacy efforts. (*Source*: Susan Kaplan, Susan Buchanan, and Debyante Porter Onduto, *Investigating Environmental Contamination: A Guide for Communities* [Great Lakes Center for Children's Environmental Health, University of Illinois Chicago School of Public Health, June 2019, updated April 2022])

GARNERING MEDIA AND PUBLIC ATTENTION

To get people's attention on any issue, it helps to start with a story and a protagonist—a parent, child, friend, or even a pet who is being threatened. When the kindergarten teacher in New York taught her students about pesticides, she noted that they can harm "people, ecosystems and even—to the 5-year-olds' horror—turtles like their class pet, Soccer Ball," according to a *New York Times* article about the effort's origin.[23] This concern spurred them to take action. And when the schoolchildren and their adult coalition partners started holding events all over the city, their presence brought attention.

Rogovin, the kids, and "an expanding circle of grown-up allies have shouted their demand in playground rallies, on the steps of City Hall, and in City Council chambers," said the *New York Times*. Whenever a hearing on the bill was scheduled, multitudinous phone calls by advocates ensured a healthy turnout of supporters. A Facebook page provided regular updates. "Join us at the public hearing for INTRO 1524," reads a post. "Rally on the steps of City Hall at 9 a.m."[24] Following the hearing, Kallos emailed residents a link to a petition to voice their support for the ban. Then, "We're getting close to banning toxic pesticides from NYC parks! We need four more Council members to sign on," with the email addresses of council members who had not yet committed.[25] And to draw in pet lovers: "Do you walk your dog in NYC parks? Chemical pesticides are sprayed in NYC parks and are toxic for pets."[26] An array of local news outlets and blogs reported on the issue and the push to get the bill brought to a vote.

Another New York advocacy campaign, which sought state funding for the network of children's environmental health centers, took a quieter but still effective approach. Advocates met twice a year, often during a yearly "legislative day" at the state capitol when they were able to meet with legislators and their staffs to describe the need for the centers. Members of the coalition also met with elected state officials in their home offices. These local meetings, according to an article describing the campaign, "were extremely valuable because they were much less hurried than meetings in the capitol, permitted more detailed conversation, and were often attended by legislators themselves" rather than staff.[27]

Along with contacting legislators, advocates can testify before school boards, local commissions like zoning and housing, city councils, state agencies, and sometimes federal agencies. A typical school board meeting, for example, will include time for members of the public to speak for several minutes. It may also be possible to get on the meeting agenda in advance in order to make a presentation about a specific issue.

Successes at the local level can provide examples for state officials. When state agencies undertake a process to develop new regulations, they are typically required to accept written comments from the public and hold a hearing upon request from a member of the public prior to making final decisions. To find out about these opportunities, sign up for mailing lists of the relevant agencies and of organizations that follow these issues and may give you a heads-up about ways to weigh in.

As the New York City schoolkids discovered, it is critical to get the attention of not only government but the general public. You can gain traction for your issue through the local news media by writing letters to the editor and opinion pieces and through social media by posting on various platforms. Whatever the medium, communicate both the health concerns associated with the issue and the benefits of the solution you are advocating, like improved school attendance or financial return on investment. Advocates can also develop written materials like fact sheets, issue briefs (which explain the importance of an issue in a page or two), and policy briefs (which describe possible policy solutions and typically recommend one in particular). These can be emailed to local or state officials, handed to them at meetings, and posted online.

For example, the Florida League of Cities communicated about its "Let Cities Work" campaign by celebrating the anniversary of the state's home rule (i.e., local authority) law. It included opinion pieces in the press, a home rule handbook for local officials, and a rally. According to the organization's executive director, these efforts throughout the state thwarted "many attempts to dilute local self-government."[28] A growing number of organizations offer tips and training on environmental health advocacy, such as the American Public Health Association's Policy Action Institute and the American College of Obstetricians and Gynecologists' "Advocate in Your State" information and tools.

Jen Walling of the Illinois Environmental Council emphasizes the importance of having a broad goal—going beyond specific issues—and of building an environmental majority in the statehouse and on city councils. She recommends a variety of tactics, including undertaking power analyses as described above, increasing media exposure on priority issues, and expanding organizational membership. "Votes are taken based on values, relationships, and beliefs," not on data, she says. "Work on having great relationships with lawmakers in lobbying efforts. Some may not support a bill now, but that can change. Keep the doors open to areas you could agree on." This openness helps to build coalitions. And, she says, use a scorecard to hold lawmakers accountable.

Success never happens immediately—and in fact it often takes years. All of those who have been in the trenches emphasize that persistence and patience are key.

Conclusion

When I started advocating for my children more than a decade ago, environmental health was not part of the popular lexicon. Now almost everyone has heard of PFAS, also known as "forever chemicals." Most people are familiar with the hazards of wildfire smoke. Residents are increasingly concerned about pollutants wafting from nearby factories. Awareness has grown.

At the same time, the gravity and expanse of these problems seem to have increased exponentially—or perhaps it is that, after years of casually using items that make our lives more convenient but also contain toxic substances, the consequences are coming home to roost. I was dismayed by the findings of a 2024 study by a group of researchers led by Jacob Gerken of Rocky Vista University College of Osteopathic Medicine and published in *Frontiers in Cancer Control and Society* that found an association between pesticide use and increased incidence of cancer equivalent to cigarette smoking. "Our findings demonstrated an association between pesticide use and increased incidence of leukemia; non-Hodgkin's lymphoma; bladder, colon, lung, and pancreatic cancer; and all cancers combined that are comparable to smoking for some cancer types," the authors wrote.[1] While ten-plus years ago I worried about how airborne pesticides were causing or worsening my son's asthma, it shouldn't be surprising that chemicals designed to kill pose hazards that go way beyond asthma. Air pollution, similarly, is now linked to impacts on most organs of the body, and even to Alzheimer's disease and other forms of dementia. Studies of the broad risks of microplastics to human health seem to be turning up almost weekly.

It all feels scary and overwhelming. And the problem goes far beyond whomever might occupy the Oval Office, or the priorities of the current EPA administrator—although these matter.

As it has gotten challenging for federal agencies to protect environmental health through new regulations, more of these initiatives have taken the form of grants, market incentives, and the like. The 2021 Bipartisan Infrastructure Act, for example, aimed to protect the environment, create jobs, and advance environmental justice by investing in built environment projects around the country. Funds addressed everything from road and bridge improvements, to broadband expansion, to replacing lead pipes that provide drinking water.

Some people I talked with for this book think this is how it should be: that the federal role should focus on supporting the states by providing them resources and funding to carry out projects that align with local priorities and needs. Some similarly believe the main federal role in protecting environmental health should be collecting data and disseminating it to states, along with providing guidance on policy and program implementation. This perspective connects with the need for more university and related training programs to better prepare state and local policymakers and researchers to collect and analyze environmental health data. This includes policy surveillance and legal epidemiology studies to better understand the policy landscape and which policies are effective in improving environmental health.

So, yes—increasingly, the future of environmental health protection in the United States appears to lie largely in states acting alone and/or in concert, while looking to each other for examples of what works and what doesn't, with (hopefully) or without significant federal support. I have mixed feelings about this. I believe the federal government should provide a strong floor of protection when it comes to environmental and occupational health, which is too important to people's lives and livelihoods to be left solely to states—some of which are poor, or lack agency staff with the requisite knowledge, or are willing to sacrifice lives and health in the name of companies that fund elected officials' political campaigns.

Still, acknowledging the rising role of states is what led me to write this book. In identifying case studies, I was determined to leapfrog over the tired, reductionist red state–blue state duality. I was gratified to find best practice policies that arose from red, blue, and purple states alike. But I am frustrated by the vast inconsistencies across states and by the lack of fundamental environmental health protections in states for which I expected better.

Overall, many states have green aspects, regardless of nomenclature used. I felt especially optimistic in identifying best-practice examples where I didn't necessarily expect to find them, like Tennessee's Livability Collaborative—even while acknowledging the gaping inconsistency that the state has not expanded Medicaid eligibility under the Affordable Care Act, a decision that poses a huge roadblock to improving health. Still, something great is happening in Tennessee.

In fact, in my research, I kept coming across fascinating nuggets from red states, which in some cases may be greener than blue states. (I continue to use these somewhat reductive terms for the sake of efficiency.) A *Science* article described how a California physician and researcher who was seeking data about COVID-19 in order to help guide the response to the virus "turned to Florida, which compared with California offer[ed] fairly detailed information" that enabled him to identify sources of transmission. (The article also points to data shortcomings in Florida, which is referred to variously as pink, red-leaning, or red.)[2] This is a particularly interesting example, since the two states were engaged in some contention over which governor was taking the most effective approach to COVID.

Another Florida example of a reddish state acting green: As a hurricane hit Florida in October 2024, "at least 2,000 Floridians found safe haven at Babcock Ranch, a community the size of Manhattan that opened in 2018 to withstand climate-driven storms," *The New York Times* reported.[3] All the structures at the ranch were built to withstand hurricane-force winds, and solar panel farms with underground transmission lines protect against electricity loss. It sounds innovative—and, at least to me, unexpected, whether in Florida or elsewhere. Also noted in the article is that the founder and president of Hunters Point, another Florida housing development built to withstand storms and prevent power loss—in this case using a solar battery–powered system—originally planned to build an RV park on the site. Instead, he pivoted to partner with the University of Central Florida and the US Green Building Council to build a net-zero house, which served as a model for the houses at Hunters Point—emphasizing the significance of these kinds of partnerships.

Similarly, a story in *Grist* about how state environmental referenda fared in the November 2024 election noted that Louisiana voters, who voted for a presidential candidate who rolled back many environmental rules in his first term, nevertheless "supported a constitutional amendment requiring federal revenue from offshore energy generation—including wind, solar, and tidal energy, in addition to oil and gas—to be placed in a fund for coastal restoration."[4] Joshua Basseches, a professor at Tulane University, told *Grist* that the Louisiana vote is "an acknowledgement that renewable and alternative energy is the future, and that even though Louisiana is an oil and gas state, it wants a part in that future." The prospect of economic and additional benefits can be persuasive even for a red, largely fossil fuel–based state. The article also quotes an environmental advocate, Justin Balik of the group Evergreen Action, who says that this and other state environmental protection initiatives on state ballots in 2024 "succeeded because they conveyed the concrete benefits of environmental action: 'What does this mean for the air that you're breathing, how does this make your energy more affordable, how does this make your community safer?'"

In another analysis, Daniel Aldana Cohen and Thea Riofrancos of the Climate and Community Institute, repeating some common critiques of the Infrastructure Act—including that it employs financial mechanisms like tax credits that are most likely to be used by companies and wealthy consumers—stress that climate protection is most effective when connected with tackling the cost-of-living crisis, and that such an agenda can be successful on the state and municipal levels.[5] A shift to less pollution that will be affordable to working- and middle-class families, they say, requires greater local and state investment in public transit and rezoning neighborhoods for greater density (to increase housing that is affordable and close to regular destinations). Again, they offer numerous red city and state examples, like (purple) Pennsylvania's "Whole Homes Repair" program that helps working-class households weatherize their homes, which lowers their utility bills. The law was enacted through the efforts of a state senator who built a coalition "that included rural voters and Republican politicians, demonstrating this kind of populism's appeal beyond party lines." While the economic analysis that demonstrates the return on investment of this kind of program may be simpler than that of New York's occupational health and children's environmental health clinics, quantifying the return on investment is again a key to success. This can be purely economic, or it can go far beyond that to examine and quantify a wide range of benefits.

So even in the absence of federal laws, there is much that states can do. It is a hopeful sign that innovative state policies stretch across the country and across states both liberal and conservative.

Every state already has some of the infrastructure described in this book's case studies, such as a university extension service. They can start there, and build. Where the foundational requirements of environmental health education and knowledge, on which all further actions depend, are lacking, advocates can find resources from other states or from national organizations and make broad use of them. Similarly, advocates for local- and state-level change can find examples of best practice policies and cost-benefit studies from other states and from a range of regional and national organizations. Many resources are available; those pushing for change in states that are farther behind need to organize and make use of them.

There will be major impediments. Especially for those who live in states that have made less progress in this area or in which polluting or toxic industries are central to the economy, industry influence will remain a potent obstacle. For example, even as state laws that preempt local pesticide policies persist, an October 2024 investigation found that contributions to state legislators by political action committees (PACs) affiliated with pesticide manufacturers have "surged" as the companies aim to achieve goals like capping court awards to people claiming harm from pesticide exposure.[6] The investigative piece, published by U.S. Right to Know, notes, "In particular, legislators in California, New Jersey, Iowa, Idaho, Illinois, Hawaii, North Carolina and Texas have benefited from the largesse of pesticide company employee political action committees during the last two years, according to data from the Federal Election Commission." Contributions at the state level from employee PACs from two such companies have quintupled in the past few years, according to the article, which lists state legislators who received such contributions and the amounts they accepted. This hurdle of industry influence reinforces Walling's suggestion to create and update scorecards to hold lawmakers accountable. In addition to their voting records, state legislators' acceptance of contributions from PACs and others that work against passing environmental health–protective legislation should be included in the scorecards.

It will take education and sustained advocacy efforts to overcome challenges like these. But I hope this book's positive case studies and recommended policy solutions can help to move state environmental health efforts forward. No one wants to suffer illness caused or contributed to by pollution, when this could be prevented. No parent wants to be awakened in the middle of the night by the sound of their child coughing and wheezing. If we want to avoid unnecessary disease, we need to make safe, healthy places for our kids and ourselves the norm; state action can go a long way to make it so.

ACKNOWLEDGMENTS

Thank you to everyone who provided input, whether via phone interview or Zoom interview, answering my follow-up questions, reviewing draft chapters, sending photographs, or all of these. One of the most enjoyable aspects of writing this book was having an excuse to talk to people around the country, including some of the giants of the field, who are moving environmental health policies forward every day. I learned something—or, more often, many things—from every single one of you. And you were all really nice!

I want to acknowledge two colleagues in particular who have made a big difference in my professional life. Peter Orris MD, MPH is a great mentor and colleague. Incredibly generous, he has gone out of his way to open doors for me, as he has for many others. And I have enormously enjoyed working with Rachel Massey ScD on a variety of projects related to toxics use reduction.

I have had the great fortune to work with many other wonderful colleagues, too numerous to name, from whom I have learned a great deal.

Thank you to Island Press senior editor Emily Turner, contributing editor Brian Romer, and the rest of the Island Press team.

This book sprung from an article I wrote for *The Conversation* website. By publishing short, straightforward articles by academics about their work, its staff aim to convey ideas from the university to the general public. Thank you to *The Conversation*'s editors for giving me an opportunity that turned out to bear major fruit.

Both of my parents, may their memory be a blessing, were excellent writers and editors who on occasion made very on-target suggestions about a sentence I should add to an essay or a magazine to which I should send my work. I thought about them as I wrote this book.

Fundamentally, I acknowledge my family. This book is really about them, especially my children and their future children—and all children. It is about my hopes for a healthy future for all.

NOTES

INTRODUCTION

1. In identifying case studies for this book, I was determined to leapfrog over the tired red state–blue state duality and choose examples from red, blue, and purple states. Nevertheless, I occasionally use these terms as shorthand.

2. IARC Working Group on the Evaluation of Carcinogenic Risks to Humans, "DDT, Lindane, and 2,4-D," *IARC Monographs on the Evaluation of Carcinogenic Risks to Humans*, no. 113 (2018), https://www.ncbi.nlm.nih.gov/books/NBK507424/.

3. National Environmental Health Association, "About," accessed June 10, 2025, https://www.neha.org/about.

4. Doug Farquhar, "Legal Framework of Environmental Public Health in the United States," in *Environmental Public Health: The Practitioner's Guide*, ed. Paul L. Knechtges, Gregory D. Kearney, and Beth A. Resnick (APHA Press, 2018).

5. I owe the phrase "from compelling to catalyzing" to Gerald Emison (see Gerald A. Emison, "From Compelling to Catalyzing: The Federal Government's Changing Role in Environmental Protection," *William & Mary Environmental Law & Policy Review* 20, no. 233 [1996], https://scholarship.law.wm.edu/wmelpr/vol20/iss2/4). Susan Kaplan, "Which State You Live in Matters for How Well Environmental Laws Protect Your Health," *The Conversation*, February 28, 2023, https://theconversation.com/which-state-you-live-in-matters-for-how-well-environmental-laws-protect-your-health-200393.

6. Frederica Perera, David Cooley, Alique Berberian, David Mills, and Patrick Kinney, "Co-Benefits to Children's Health of the U.S. Regional Greenhouse Gas Initiative," *Environmental Health Perspectives* 128, no. 7 (July 29, 2020), https://doi.org/10.1289/EHP6706.

7. Office of the Attorney General, Commonwealth of Massachusetts, "A.G. Healey Calls on U.S. Senate to Pass Legislation to Protect the Public from Highly Toxic 'Forever' Chemicals," November 9, 2022, https://www.mass.gov/news/ag-healey-calls-on-us-senate-to-pass-legislation-to-protect-the-public-from-highly-toxic-forever-chemicals.

8. Ed Yong, "America Is Zooming Through the Pandemic Panic-Neglect Cycle," *The Atlantic*, March 17, 2022, https://www.theatlantic.com/health/archive/2022/03/congress-covid-spending-bill/627090/.

CHAPTER 1

1. US Environmental Protection Agency, "Federal Insecticide, Fungicide, and Rodenticide Act (FIFRA) and Federal Facilities," February 15, 2024, https://www.epa.gov/enforcement/federal-insecticide-fungicide-and-rodenticide-act-fifra-and-federal-facilities. See also Danica Li, "Toxic Spring: The Capriciousness of Cost-Benefit Analysis Under FIFRA's Pesticide Registration Process and Its Effect on Farmworkers," *California Law Review* 103, no. 5 (October 2015): 1405–47, https://www.jstor.org/stable/24758543.
2. Nathan Donley, "The U.S. Lags Behind Other Agricultural Nations in Banning Harmful Pesticides," *Environmental Health* 18 (2019): 44, https://doi.org/10.1186/s12940-019-0488-0.
3. Bob Weinhold, "Mystery in a Bottle: Will the EPA Require Public Disclosure of Inert Pesticide Ingredients?," *Environmental Health Perspectives* 118, no. 4 (April 2010): A168–71, https://doi.org/10.1289/ehp.118-a168.
4. Christina Jewett and Julie Creswell, "California's Ban on Red Food Dye Puts F.D.A.'s Food Policies on the Spot," *The New York Times*, October 14, 2023, https://www.nytimes.com/2023/10/14/health/california-ban-red-dye-food.html.
5. Christina Jewett and Will Fitzgibbon, "Lead-Tainted Applesauce Sailed Through Gaps in Food-Safety System," *The New York Times*, February 27, 2024, https://www.nytimes.com/2024/02/27/world/europe/lead-applesauce-food-safety.html.
6. Paul L. Knechtges, "Historical Overview of Professionalism in Environmental Public Health," in *Environmental Public Health: The Practitioner's Guide*, ed. Paul L. Knechtges, Gregory D. Kearney, and Beth A. Resnick (APHA Press, 2018).
7. Knechtges, "Historical Overview."
8. Interview with Thomas Burke, February 5, 2024.
9. Institute of Medicine, *The Future of Public Health* (National Academies Press, 1988), 13.
10. Beth A. Resnick, "Organization of Environmental Public Health," in *Environmental Public Health: The Practitioner's Guide*.
11. Interview with Thomas Burke, February 5, 2024.
12. Knechtges, "Historical Overview."
13. Thomas A. Burke, Nadia M. Shalauta, Nga L. Tran, and Barry S. Stern, "The Environmental Web: A National Profile of the State Infrastructure for Environ-

mental Health and Protection," *Journal of Public Health Management and Practice* 3, no. 2 (March 1997): 1–12, https://www.jstor.org/stable/44967635.

14. Megan Wallace and Joshua M. Sharfstein, "The Patchwork U.S. Public Health System," *New England Journal of Medicine* 386, no. 1 (January 6, 2022): 1–4, https://doi.org/10.1056/NEJMp2104881.

15. Kate Ackley, "U.S. Chamber of Commerce Dips to Second Place in K Street Spending," *Roll Call*, January 23, 2023, https://rollcall.com/2023/01/23/u-s-chamber-dips-to-second-place-in-k-street-spending/.

16. Michelle Boone, Christine A. Bishop, Leigh A. Boswell, Robert D. Brodman, Joanna Burger, Carlos Davidson, et al., "Pesticide Regulation Amid the Influence of Industry," *BioScience* 64, no. 10 (October 2014): 917, https://doi.org/10.1093/biosci/biu138.

17. Boone et al., "Pesticide Regulation," 918.

18. Rina Kuusipalo, "Proposition 65: The Invisible Revolution in Toxic Chemicals Regulation," Stanford Law School Blogs, March 10, 2017, https://law.stanford.edu/2017/03/10/proposition-65-the-invisible-revolution-in-toxic-chemicals-regulation/.

19. US Centers for Disease Control and Prevention, "Preemption of Local Public Health Laws," accessed April 20, 2024, https://www.cdc.gov/phlp/docs/preemption-issue-brief.pdf.

20. Emily Newburger, "'Why Is It So Hard to Make Environmental Law?,'" *Harvard Law Today*, April 18, 2023, https://hls.harvard.edu/today/why-is-it-so-hard-to-make-environmental-law/.

21. Sam Becker, "Government Shutdown Threats Are Becoming More Common. Blame TV, Social Media, and Newt Gingrich," *Fast Company*, November 16, 2023, https://www.fastcompany.com/90984129/government-shutdowns-more-common-over-time-tv-social-media.

22. John Larsen, Ben King, and Maggie Young, "Has the Supreme Court Blocked the Path to the 2030 Climate Target?," The Rhodium Group (blog), July 1, 2022, https://rhg.com/research/supreme-court-2030-climate-target.

23. Kenneth Olden, "The EPA: Time to Re-Invent Environmental Protection," *American Journal of Public Health* 108, no. 4 (April 2018): 454–56, https://doi.org/10.2105/AJPH.2017.304303.

CHAPTER 2

1. Lex Harvey, "California Overtakes Japan to Become the World's Fourth-Largest Economy," *CNN*, April 25, 2025, https://www.cnn.com/2025/04/25/business/california-japan-economy-tariffs-intl-hnk.

2. Nicholas Bryner and Meredith Hankins, "Why California Gets to Write Its Own Auto Emissions Standards: 5 Questions Answered," *The Conversation*, April 6, 2018, https://theconversation.com/why-california-gets-to-write-its-own-auto-emissions-standards-5-questions-answered-94379.

3. California Air Resources Board, "Zero-Emission Vehicle Program—About," 2024, https://ww2.arb.ca.gov/our-work/programs/zero-emission-vehicle-program/about.

4. San Francisco Environment Department, "San Francisco Reduced-Risk Pesticide List 2024," accessed February 17, 2024, https://www.sfenvironment.org/san-francisco-reduced-risk-pesticide-list.

5. James P. Lester and Emmett N. Lombard, "The Comparative Analysis of State Environmental Policy," *Natural Resources Journal* 30, no. 2 (Spring 1990): 301–19.

6. Lester and Lombard, "Comparative Analysis."

7. Joshua A. Basseches, Rebecca Bromley-Trujillo, Maxwell T. Boykoff, Trevor Culhane, Galen Hall, Noel Healy, et al., "Climate Policy Conflict in the U.S. States: A Critical Review and Way Forward," *Climatic Change* 170 (2022): art. 32, https://doi.org/10.1007/s10584-022-03319-w.

8. Basseches et al., "Climate Policy Conflict."

9. Basseches et al., "Climate Policy Conflict."

10. David J. Hess, Quan D. Mai, and Kate Pride Brown, "Red States, Green Laws: Ideology and Renewable Energy Legislation in the United States," *Energy Research & Social Science* 11 (2016): 19–28.

11. Debra Kahn, Bruce Ritchie, Ry Rivard, and Mike Lee, "Don't Call It Climate Change. Red States Prepare for 'Extreme Weather,'" *Politico*, November 25, 2021, https://www.politico.com/states/california/story/2021/11/23/adapting-to-climate-is-a-winning-issue-for-politicians-even-in-red-states-1394620.

12. US Centers for Disease Control and Prevention, "National Environmental Public Health Tracking," November 3, 2022, https://www.cdc.gov/nceh/tracking/.

13. Interview with Thomas Burke, February 5, 2024.

14. US Centers for Disease Control and Prevention, "Florida's Success," March 2, 2018, accessed January 25, 2024, https://www.cdc.gov/nceh/tracking/success/florida.htm.

15. Mary A. Fox, Sheriza Baksh, Juleen Lam, and Beth Resnick, "Building the Future of Environmental Public Health Tracking: Proceedings and Recommendations of an Expert Panel Workshop," *Journal of Environmental Health* 79, no. 10 (June 2017): 14-9.

16. Susan Kaplan, "Which State You Live in Matters for How Well Environmental Laws Protect Your Health," *The Conversation*, February 28, 2023, https://theconversation.com/which-state-you-live-in-matters-for-how-well-environmental-laws-protect-your-health-200393.

17. Frederica Perera, David Cooley, Alique Berberian, David Mills, and Patrick Kinney, "Co-Benefits to Children's Health of the U.S. Regional Greenhouse Gas Initiative," *Environmental Health Perspectives* 128, no. 7 (July 29, 2020), https://doi.org/10.1289/EHP6706.

18. David E. Jacobs, Tom Kelly, and John Sobolewski, "Linking Public Health, Housing, and Indoor Environmental Policy: Successes and Challenges at Local and Federal Agencies in the United States," *Environmental Health Perspectives* 115, no. 6 (January 25, 2007): 976–82, https://ehp.niehs.nih.gov/doi/10.1289/ehp.8990.

19. Jacobs et al., "Linking Public Health."

20. US Environmental Protection Agency (EPA), "Organophosphate Insecticides," in *Recognition and Management of Pesticide Poisonings*, 6th ed. (2013), https://www.epa.gov/sites/default/files/documents/rmpp_6thed_ch5_organophosphates.pdf.

21. Leonardo Trasande, "When Enough Data Are Not Enough to Enact Policy: The Failure to Ban Chlorpyrifos," *PLOS Biology* 15, no. 12 (December 21, 2017), https://doi.org/10.1371/journal.pbio.2003671.

22. EPA, "Organophosphate Insecticides."

23. Interview with Thomas Burke, February 5, 2024.

24. Association of Public and Land-Grant Universities Board on Agriculture Assembly, "Land-Grant Impacts," 2024, https://landgrantimpacts.org/extension/.

CHAPTER 3

1. Commonwealth of Massachusetts, "About the Toxics Use Reduction Act (TURA) Program," accessed December 3, 2024, https://www.mass.gov/guides/about-the-toxics-use-reduction-act-tura-program#-tura-program-agencies-and-services.

2. Commonwealth of Massachusetts, "About the Toxics Use Reduction Act (TURA) Program."

3. Commonwealth of Massachusetts, "About the Toxics Use Reduction Act (TURA) Program."

4. Commonwealth of Massachusetts, "About the Toxics Use Reduction Act (TURA) Program."

5. Michael Ellenbecker and Ken Geiser, "At the Source: The Origins of the Massachusetts Toxics Use Reduction Program and an Overview of This Special Issue," *Journal of Cleaner Production* 19, no. 5 (2011): 389–96, https://doi.org/10.1016/j.jclepro.2010.10.018.

6. Ellenbecker and Geiser, "At the Source."

7. Ellenbecker and Geiser, "At the Source."

8. Toxics Use Reduction Institute, "Massachusetts Toxics Use Reduction Act," June 2018, https://www.turi.org/wp-content/uploads/2024/03/TURAOverview.June 2018.pdf.

9. Commonwealth of Massachusetts, Executive Office of Energy and Environmental Affairs, Department of Environmental Protection, "Reporting Year 2021 Toxics Use Reduction Information Release," July 2023, https://malegislature .gov/Bills/193/SD2696.pdf.

10. National Cancer Institute, "Trichloroethylene (TCE)," December 8, 2022, https: //www.cancer.gov/about-cancer/causes-prevention/risk/substances/trichloroethy lene.

11. Jason P. Marshall, "Hands-On Assistance Improves Already Successful Pollution Prevention Services of the Toxics Use Reduction Institute's Laboratory," *Journal of Cleaner Production* 19, no. 5 (March 2011): 424–28, https://doi.org/10.1016/j .jclepro.2010.05.020.

12. Rachel I. Massey, Heather Tenney, and Elizabeth Harriman, "Higher Hazard Substances Under the Massachusetts Toxics Use Reduction Act: Lessons from the First Four Years," *New Solutions* 21, no. 3 (2011): 457–76, https://doi.org /10.2190/NS.21.3.k

13. Massey et al., "Higher Hazard Substances."

14. Rachel I. Massey, "Program Assessment at the 20 Year Mark: Experiences of Massachusetts Companies and Communities with the Toxics Use Reduction Act (TURA) Program," *Journal of Cleaner Production* 19, no. 5 (2011): 505–16, https://doi.org/10.1016/j.jclepro.2010.08.011.

15. Massey, "Program Assessment."

16. Massey, "Program Assessment."

17. Toxics Use Reduction Institute and Office of Technical Assistance and Technology, "Toxics Use Reduction and Resource Conservation: Competitiveness Impacts for Massachusetts Businesses," TURI Report #2017-002, September 2017.

18. Toxics Use Reduction Institute, "Toxics Use Reduction."

19. Toxics Use Reduction Institute, "Toxics Use Reduction."

20. Ellenbecker and Geiser, "At the Source."

21. Michael P. Wilson et al., "Green Chemistry in California: A Framework for Leadership in Chemicals Policy and Innovation," *New Solutions* 16, no. 4 (2006): 365–72, https://doi.org/10.2190/9584-1330-1647-136P, cited in Massey, "Program Assessment."

22. Massachusetts Office of Technical Assistance for Toxics Use Reduction, "The Effect of Providing On-Site Technical Assistance for Toxics Use Reduction," July 2006, https://www.mass.gov/doc/the-effect-of-providing-on-site-technical- assistance-for-toxics-use-reduction/download.

23. Dara O'Rourke and Eungkyoon Lee, "Mandatory Planning for Environmental Innovation: Evaluating Regulatory Mechanisms for Toxics Use Reduction," *Journal of Environmental Planning and Management* 47, no. 2 (March 2004): 181–200, https://doi.org/10.1080/0964056042000209111.

24. O'Rourke and Lee, "Mandatory Planning."

25. Interview with Janet Hurley, April 1, 2024.

26. Texas Department of Agriculture, "School Integrated Pest Management (IPM)," accessed January 11, 2024, https://www.texasagriculture.gov/Regulatory-Pro grams/Pesticides/Structural-Pest-Control-Service/School-Integrated-Pest-Man agement.

27. Gabe Saldana, "How Texas Became Leader in Safe Public School Pest Management," *AgriLife Today*, September 10, 2020, https://agrilifetoday.tamu.edu/2020 /09/10/how-texas-became-leader-in-safe-public-school-pest-management/.

28. Texas A&M University, "History of School IPM Program in Texas," accessed January 11, 2024, https://extensionentomology.tamu.edu/wp-content/uploads /sites/8/2011/08/History-of-School-IPM-Program-in-Texas.pdf.

29. Texas A&M University, "History of School IPM Program."

30. Janet Hurley, Michael Merchant, Charles Allen, Dean McCorkle, and Dan Hanselka, "Overview of the School IPM Program in Texas," Texas A&M Agri-Life Extension Service, February 2013, https://ipm.tamu.edu/files/2013/02 /School-IPM-White-paper-Final.pdf.

31. Hurley et al., "Overview of the School IPM Program."

32. Texas A&M AgriLife Extension, "IPM Cost Calculator," accessed April 10, 2024, https://ipmcalculator.com/. It was developed by the Southwest Technical Resource Center for School IPM and collaborating states with financial support from the US Department of Agriculture's Southern Region IPM program.

33. Interview with Janet Hurley, April 1, 2024.

34. Occupations Code—Texas Structural Pest Control Act, accessed April 10, 2024, https://statutes.capitol.texas.gov/Docs/OC/htm/OC.1951.htm.

35. Texas A&M University, "History of School IPM Program in Texas."

36. Massey, "Program Assessment."

37. Minnesota Department of Health, "Chemicals of High Concern," January 2, 2024, https://www.health.state.mn.us/communities/environment/childenvhealth /tfka/highconcern.html; Maine Department of Environmental Protection, "Safer Chemicals," accessed June 7, 2024, https://www.maine.gov/dep/safechem/.

38. State of Washington Department of Ecology, "Cost Analysis for Pollution Prevention," May 2022, https://apps.ecology.wa.gov/publications/documents/2204 025.pdf.

39. Pamela Eliason and Gregory Morose, "Safer Alternatives Assessment: The Massachusetts Process as a Model for State Governments," *Journal of Cleaner Produc-*

tion 19, no. 5 (2011): 517–26, https://doi.org/10.1016/j.jclepro.2010.05 .011.

40. Eliason and Morose, "Safer Alternatives Assessment."

41. Interstate Chemicals Clearinghouse, "Mission & History," accessed June 8, 2024, https://www.theic2.org/about/mission-history/.

42. Jesse Wagner, Tim F. Morse, and Nancy Simcox, "Estimated Chemical Usage by Manufacturers in Connecticut," *Journal of Cleaner Production* 19, no. 5 (2011): 527–31, https://doi.org/10.1016/j.jclepro.2010.06.011.

43. Donald G. Chittock and Kenneth F.D. Hughey, "A Review of International Practice in the Design of Voluntary Pollution Prevention Programs," *Journal of Cleaner Production* 19, no. 5 (2011): 542–51, https://doi.org/10.1016/j.jclepro .2010.03.015.

44. Kenneth F.D. Hughey and Donald G. Chittock, "Voluntary Pollution Prevention Programs in New Zealand—An Evaluation of Practice Versus Design Features," *Journal of Cleaner Production* 19, no. 5 (2011): 532–41, https://doi.org /10.1016/j.jclepro.2010.03.010.

45. US Environmental Protection Agency, "IPM in Schools—Model Pesticide Safety and IPM Guidance Policy for School Districts," last updated June 26, 2024, https://www.epa.gov/ipm/ipm-schools-model-pesticide-safety-and-ipm-guidance -policy-school-districts.

46. Xerces Society for Invertebrate Conservation, "Reducing Pesticide Use & Impacts," accessed June 7, 2024, https://www.xerces.org/pesticides.

CHAPTER 4

1. Carly R. Levy, Lynelle M. Phillips, Carolyn J. Murray, Lindsay A. Tallon, and Rosemary M. Caron, "Addressing Gaps in Public Health Education to Advance Environmental Justice: Time for Action," *American Journal of Public Health* 12, no. 1 (January 2022): 69–74, https://www.ncbi.nlm.nih.gov/pmc/articles/PMC8713638/.

2. US Government Accountability Office, "Workplace Safety and Health: Multiple Challenges Lengthen OSHA's Standard Setting," April 2012, https://www.gao .gov/assets/gao-12-330.pdf.

3. David Michaels, "Is OSHA Working for Working People?," Statement before the Subcommittee on Employment & Workplace Safety, US Senate Committee on Health, Education, Labor & Pensions, April 26, 2007.

4. Steven B. Markowitz, Ellen Fischer, Marianne C. Fahs, Judy Shapiro, and Philip J. Landrigan, "Occupational Disease in New York State: A Comprehensive Examination," *Journal of Industrial Medicine* 16 (1989): 417–35.

5. New York State Department of Health, "New York State Occupational Health Clinics Oversight Committee: Report to the Governor and Legislature—Public Review Draft," July 2012, https://www.health.ny.gov/environmental/workplace /occupational_health_clinic/oversight_committee_report.htm.

6. New York State Department of Health, "The New York State Prevention Agenda 2019–2024: An Overview," April 27, 2021, https://www.health.ny.gov/preven tion/prevention_agenda/2019–2024/docs/ship/overview.pdf.

7. Rafael E. de la Hoz, Mathew London, George Friedman-Jiménez, and William N. Rom, "Occupational and Environmental Medicine in New York State," *International Archives of Occupational and Environmental Health* 70 (1997): 1–8, https://doi.org/10.1007/s004200050180; Michael Lax, "New York State's COSH Movement: A Brief History," *New Solutions* 28, no. 2 (2018): 202–26, https: //ohccupstate.org/index_htm_files/published%20Lax%202018_1.pdf.

8. De la Hoz et al., "Occupational and Environmental Medicine."

9. De la Hoz et al., "Occupational and Environmental Medicine."

10. De la Hoz et al., "Occupational and Environmental Medicine."

11. De la Hoz et al., "Occupational and Environmental Medicine."

12. Interview with Michael Lax, April 19, 2024.

13. New York State Department of Health, "New York State Occupational Health Clinics Oversight Committee."

14. Michael B. Lax and Jeanette M. Zoeckler, *Occupational Disease in New York State: An Update* (Occupational Health Clinical Center, SUNY Upstate Medical University, September 2021), https://ohccupstate.org/index_htm_files/Occupa tional%20Disease%20in%20NYS%20Lax%20Zoeckler%20Dec%202021 .pdf.

15. Mount Sinai Children's Environmental Health Center and PEHSU, "Centers of Excellence in Children's Environmental Health," undated. Provided by Philip J. Landrigan.

16. Philip J. Landrigan, "Public Policy on Children's Environmental Health in the United States" (unpublished chapter).

17. Maida Galvez, Geoffrey Collins, Robert W. Amler, Allen Dozor, Evonne Kaplan-Liss, Joel Forman, et al., "Building New York State Centers of Excellence in Children's Environmental Health: A Replicable Model in a Time of Uncertainty," *American Journal of Public Health* 109 (2018): 108–12, https://doi.org /10.2105/AJPH.2018.304742.

18. New York State Children's Environmental Health Centers (NYSCHECK), "Who We Are and What We Do," accessed December 18, 2024, https://nyscheck.org /about/.

19. NYSCHECK, "Who We Are."

20. NYSCHECK, "New York State Prescriptions for Prevention—English," accessed December 18, 2024, https://nyscheck.org/rx/.

21. NYSCHECK, "Annual Report: 2022–2023," accessed March 2024, https://nyscheck.org/wp-content/uploads/2024/04/2022-23-NYSCHECK-ANNUAL-REPORT.pdf.

22. NYSCHECK, "Case Studies," accessed December 17, 2024, https://nyscheck.org/case-studies/.

23. "The Need for Centers of Excellence in Children's Environmental Health in New York State," March 11, 2008 (provided by Philip J. Landrigan).

24. Galvez et al., "Building New York State Centers of Excellence."

25. Pennsylvania Department of Health, *Chemical Exposures and Health Outcomes of the East Palestine, Ohio Train Derailment on Pennsylvania First Responders* (May 2023), https://www.pa.gov/content/dam/copapwp-pagov/en/health/documents/topics/documents/environmental-health/Report_Chemical%20Exposures%20and%20Health%20Outcomes%20-%20East%20Palestine%20Ohio.pdf.

26. National Academies, "Public Health Research and Surveillance Priorities from the East Palestine Train Derailment: Proceedings of a Workshop—in Brief," 2024, https://nap.nationalacademies.org/read/27441/chapter/1.

CHAPTER 5

1. Yanelli Nunez, Jaime Benavides, Jenni A. Shearston, Elena M. Krieger, Misbath Daouda, Lucas R. F. Henneman, et al., "An Environmental Justice Analysis of Air Pollution Emissions in the United States from 1970 to 2010," *Nature Communication* 15, no. 268 (2024): 1–13, https://doi.org/10.1038/s41467-023-43492-9.

2. Paul Mohai, Paula M. Lantz, Jeffrey Morenoff, James S. House, and Richard P. Mero, "Racial and Socioeconomic Disparities in Residential Proximity to Polluting Industrial Facilities: Evidence from the Americans' Changing Lives Study," *American Journal of Public Health* 99, no. S3 (November 2009): S649–56, https://doi.org/10.2105/AJPH.2007.131383.

3. US Department of Health and Human Services, "Environmental Justice," accessed May 4, 2023, https://www.hhs.gov/civil-rights/for-individuals/special-topics/environmental-justice/index.html.

4. Dollie Burwell and Luke W. Cole, "Environmental Justice Comes Full Circle: Warren County Before and After," *Golden Gate University Environmental Law Journal* 1, no. 1 (January 2007), https://digitalcommons.law.ggu.edu/gguelj/vol1/iss1/4/.

5. Burwell and Cole, "Environmental Justice Comes Full Circle."

6. Burwell and Cole, "Environmental Justice Comes Full Circle."
7. United Church of Christ, *Toxic Wastes and Race in the United States: A National Report on the Racial and Socio-Economic Characteristics of Communities with Hazardous Waste Sites* (Commission for Racial Justice, United Church of Christ, 1987), https://www.ucc.org/wp-content/uploads/2020/12/ToxicWastesRace.pdf.
8. US Government Accountability Office, "Environmental Justice: Federal Efforts Need Better Planning, Coordination, and Methods to Assess Progress," September 16, 2019, https://www.gao.gov/products/gao-19-543.
9. The White House, "Justice40," accessed August 23, 2024, https://www.whitehouse.gov/environmentaljustice/justice40/.
10. Nathan Donley, Robert D. Bullard, Jeannie Economos, Iris Figueroa, Jovita Lee, Amy K. Liebman, et al., "Pesticides and Environmental Injustice in the U.S.A.: Root Causes, Current Regulatory Reinforcement and a Path Forward," *BMC Public Health* 22, no.708 (2022), https://doi.org/10.1186/s12889-022-13057-4.
11. Donley et al., "Pesticides and Environmental Injustice."
12. Donley et al., "Pesticides and Environmental Injustice."
13. Manann Donoghoe, Andre M. Perry, and Hannah Stephens, "The U.S. Can't Achieve Environmental Justice Through One-Size-Fits-All Climate Policy," Brookings, June 1, 2023, https://www.brookings.edu/articles/the-us-cant-achieve-environmental-justice-through-one-size-fits-all-climate-policy/.
14. Donoghoe et al., "The U.S. Can't Achieve Environmental Justice."
15. Uma Outka, "Federal-State Conflicts Over Environmental Justice—Parts I and II," Center for Progressive Reform, November 13, 2023, https://progressivereform.org/cpr-blog/federal-state-conflicts-over-environmental-justice/. Also see Hannah Perls, "Breaking Down the Environmental Justice Provisions in the 2022 Inflation Reduction Act," Harvard Law School Environmental & Energy Law Program, August 12, 2022, https://eelp.law.harvard.edu/ira-ej-provisions/.
16. George Alexeeff, John Faust, Laura Meehan August, Carmen Milanes, Karen Randles, and Lauren Zeise, *Cumulative Impacts: Building a Scientific Foundation* (California Office of Environmental Health Hazard Assessment, December 2010), https://oehha.ca.gov/media/downloads/calenviroscreen/report/cireport123110.pdf.
17. Alexeeff et al., *Cumulative Impacts.*
18. Laura August, Komal Bangia, Laurel Plummer, Shankar Prasad, Kelsey Ranjbar, Andrew Slocombe, and Walker Wieland, *CalEnviroScreen 4.0* (California Office of Environmental Health Hazard Assessment, October 2021), https://oehha.ca.gov/media/downloads/calenviroscreen/report/calenviroscreen40reportf2021.pdf.
19. Alexeeff et al., "Cumulative Impacts."

20. Alexeeff et al., "Cumulative Impacts."

21. Alexeeff et al., "Cumulative Impacts."

22. California Office of Environmental Health Hazard Assessment, "Scoring & Model: What Is the CalEnviroScreen Model?," accessed July 15, 2024, https://oehha.ca.gov/calenviroscreen/scoring-model.

23. California Air Resources Board, "History," accessed July 15, 2024, https://ww2.arb.ca.gov/about/history.

24. LegiScan, California Assembly Bill 617, https://legiscan.com/CA/text/AB617/id/1642678.

25. LegiScan, California Assembly Bill 617.

26. California Air Resources Board, *Community Air Protection Blueprint* (October 2018), https://www.sdapcd.org/content/dam/sdapcd/documents/capp/Community-Air-Protection-Blueprint-October-2018.pdf.

27. Rachel Becker, "Has California's Landmark Law Cleaned Communities' Dirty Air?," *CalMatters*, January 31, 2022, https://calmatters.org/environment/2022/01/california-air-quality-environmental-justice-law/.

28. Deborah Behles, *Lessons from California's Community Emissions Reduction Plans: AB 617's Flawed Implementation Must Not Be Repeated* (California Environmental Justice Alliance, n.d.), https://caleja.org/wp-content/uploads/2021/05/CEJA_AB617_r4-2.pdf

29. Behles, *Lessons from California's Community Emissions Reduction Plans.*

30. Kay Cuajunco and Amy Vanderwarker, *Green Zones Across California* (California Environmental Justice Alliance, n.d.), https://ceja.org/wp-content/uploads/2015/09/GREENZONES.2015.30MB.pdf; "Case Study: National City's Amortization Ordinance," California Green Zones—A California Environmental Justice Alliance Initiative, accessed August 23, 2024, https://calgreenzones.org/case-study-national-citys-amortization-ordinance/.

31. Cuajunco and Vanderwarker, *Green Zones Across California.*

32. See California Air Resources Board, "UC Davis AB 617 Engagement Studies and Convening Materials," accessed July 2, 2024, https://ww2.arb.ca.gov/capp/cst/rdi/uc-davis-ab-617-engagement-studies-and-convening-materials.

33. California Air Resources Board, "Wilmington, Carson, West Long Beach," accessed August 23, 2024, https://ww2.arb.ca.gov/our-work/programs/community-air-protection-program/communityhub-2-0/wilmington-carson-west-long.

34. Jonathan K. London, Peter Nguyen, Mia Dawson, and Katrina Manrique, *Community Engagement in AB 617: An Evaluation of Challenges, Successes, Lessons Learned and Recommendations for the Future* (University of California Davis, June 2020), https://ww2.arb.ca.gov/sites/default/files/2020-10/17RD035%20-%20English%20-%20AB%20617%20UC%20Davis%20Report%20Final%20for%20distribution.pdf. Also see Lily MacIver, Jonathan London, Natalie Samp-

son, Margaret Gordon, Richard Grow, and Veronica Eady, "West Oakland's Experience in Building Community Power to Confront Environmental Injustice Through California's Assembly Bill 617," *American Journal of Public Health* 112, no. 2 (February 1, 2022): 262–70, https://doi.org/10.2105/AJPH.2021.306 592.

35. California Air Resources Board, "2022-Assembly Bill 1749 (Garcia, Cristina), Community Emissions Reduction Programs: Toxic Air Contaminants and Criteria Air Pollutants (Chaptered)," accessed August 12, 2024, https://ww2.arb .ca.gov/2022-assembly-bill-1749-garcia-cristina-community-emissions-reduc tion-programs-toxic-air.

36. California Air Resources Board (CARB), *Community Air Protection Blueprint 2.0* (October 2023), https://ww2.arb.ca.gov/sites/default/files/2024-04/BP2.0 _FULL_FINAL_ENG_2024_04_09.pdf.

37. CARB, *Community Air Protection Blueprint 2.0.*

38. CARB, *Community Air Protection Blueprint 2.0.*

39. CARB, *Community Air Protection Blueprint 2.0.*

40. California EPA, "CalEnviroScreen 10th Anniversary," May 16, 2023, https: //storymaps.arcgis.com/stories/413d2b6be94c42ce85ada08499623a2a/.

41. CARB, *Community Air Protection Blueprint 2.0.*

42. London et al., "Community Engagement in AB 617."

43. California Air Resources Board, "Outline of Measurement Technologies," accessed October 14, 2024, https://ww2.arb.ca.gov/capp-resource-center/commu nity-air-monitoring/outline-of-measurement-technologies.

44. San Joaquin Valley Air Pollution Control District, "Community Air Monitoring," accessed October 14, 2024, https://community.valleyair.org/community -air-monitoring.

45. London et al., "Community Engagement in AB 617."

46. Charles Lee, "Another Game Changer in the Making? Lessons from States Advancing Environmental Justice Through Mapping and Cumulative Impact Strategies," *Environmental Law Reporter* 51 (August 2021), https://www.elr.info /sites/default/files/article/2021/07/51.10676.pdf.

47. Lee, "Another Game Changer?"

CHAPTER 6

1. National Association of County & City Health Officials (NACCHO), "Health in All Policies," accessed June 20, 2024, https://www.naccho.org/programs /community-health/healthy-community-design/health-in-all-policies.

2. NACCHO, "Health in All Policies."

3. Association of State and Territorial Health Officials, *Health in All Policies: A Framework for State Health Leadership* (2018), https://www.astho.org/globalassets/pdf/hiap/health-in-all-policies-framework.pdf.

4. Physical Activity Alliance, "Commentaries on Physical Activity and Health: Tackling Health on all Fronts in Tennessee. A Conversation with Leslie Meehan, Director of Primary Prevention at the Tennessee Department of Health," accessed June 20, 2024, https://paamovewithus.org/tackling-health-on-all-fronts-in-tennessee/.

5. Physical Activity Alliance, "Commentaries on Physical Activity."

6. John Vick, *Tennessee Livability Collaborative: Evaluation Report* (August 2019), https://www.tn.gov/content/dam/tn/health/program-areas/primary-prevention/TLC%20Evaluation%20Report%202019.pdf.

7. Vick, *Tennessee Livability Collaborative.*

8. Colorado Association of Local Public Health Officials, "Colorado's Public Health System . . . and a Bit of History," accessed January 16, 2025, https://www.calpho.org/uploads/6/8/7/2/68728279/co_public_health_history.pdf.

9. Colorado Department of Public Health and Environment, "CHAPS Background and Requirements," accessed January 10, 2025, https://cdphe-lpha.colorado.gov/assessment-and-planning/chaps-background-and-requirements.

10. Public Health Accreditation Board, "Colorado Department of Public Health & Environment," accessed January 14, 2025, https://phaboard.org/resources/cdphe/.

11. "Sustaining Equitable Outcomes via Partnerships, Policy, and Practice," PHNCI and NORC at the University of Chicago, February 2019, https://phaboard.org/wp-content/uploads/PHNCI-Case-Study-Colorado.pdf.

12. Public Health Accreditation Board, "Colorado Department of Public Health & Environment."

13. State of Colorado, "Colorado Climate Action," accessed January 10, 2025, https://climate.colorado.gov/contact-experts.

14. Public Health Accreditation Board, "Colorado Department of Public Health & Environment."

15. William Mundo, Peter Manetta, Meredith P. Fort, and Angela Sauaia, "A Qualitative Study of Health in All Policies at the Local Level," *INQUIRY: The Journal of Health Care Organization, Provision, and Financing* 56 (2019), https://doi.org/10.1177/0046958019874153.

16. Dawn Pepin, Benjamin D. Winig, Derek Carr, and Peter D. Jacobson, "Collaborating for Health: Health in All Policies and the Law," *Journal of Law and Medical Ethics* 45, no. 1 (March 2017): 60–64, https://doi.org/10.1177/1073110517703327.

17. For example, see City of Lauderhill, Florida, "Lauderhill Health and Prosperity Partnership," accessed June 22, 2024, https://www.lauderhill-fl.gov/commission /commissioner-melissa-p-dunn/lauderhill-health-and-prosperity-partnership.

18. Pepin et al., "Collaborating for Health."

19. Vermont Department of Health, "Health in All Policies," last updated April 9, 2024, https://www.healthvermont.gov/about/our-vision-mission-values/health -all-policies.

20. Pepin et al., "Collaborating for Health."

21. Association of State and Territorial Health Officials (ASTHO), "Making the Connection Between Health in All Policies and State Health Improvement Plans," May 3, 2023, https://www.astho.org/topic/report/making-the-connection -between-hiap-and-ship/.

22. ASTHO, "Making the Connection."

23. ASTHO, "Making the Connection."

24. ChangeLab Solutions, "Commitment to Change: Health in All Policies Model Policies," accessed January 12, 2025, https://www.changelabsolutions.org/prod uct/commitment-change.

25. Peter D. Jacobson, "Promoting Health Equity Through Health in All Policies Programs: A Health Law Perspective," Harvard Law School Petrie-Flom Center, July 22, 2018, https://blog.petrieflom.law.harvard.edu/2018/07/22/pro moting-health-equity-through-health-in-all-policies-programs-a-health-law -perspective/.

26. Richard L. Hall and Peter D. Jacobson, "Examining Whether the Health-in-All-Policies Approach Promotes Health Equity," *Health Affairs* 37, no. 3 (2018): 364–70.

27. Public Health Accreditation Board, "Colorado Department of Public Health & Environment."

28. NACCHO, CDC, and ASTHO, "Health in All Policies Evaluation Tool for State and Local Health Departments," July 25, 2024, https://www.astho.org /topic/resource/health-in-all-policies-evaluation-tool/.

29. Vermont Department of Health, "Health in All Policies."

CHAPTER 7

1. XiaoZhi Lim, "Do We Know Enough About the Safety of Quat Disinfectants?," *Chemical & Engineering News*, August 2, 2020, https://cen.acs.org/safety/con sumer-safety/know-enough-safety-quat-disinfectants/98/i30.

2. Jose L. Jimenez, Linsey C. Marr, Katherine Randall, Edward Thomas Ewing, Zeynep Tufekci, Trish Greenhalgh, et al., "What Were the Historical Reasons for

the Resistance to Recognizing Airborne Transmission During the COVID-19 Pandemic?," *Indoor Air*, August 21, 2022, https://doi.org/10.1111/ina.13070.

3. Jimenez et al., "What Were the Historical Reasons?"

4. Jimenez et al., "What Were the Historical Reasons?"

5. Raffaele Marfella, Francesco Prattichizzo, Celestino Sardu, Gianluca Fulgenzi, Laura Graciotti, Tatiana Spadoni, et al., "Microplastics and Nanoplastics in Atheromas and Cardiovascular Events," *New England Journal of Medicine* 390 (2024): 900–910.

6. Minghui Li, Zongkun Hou, Run Meng, Shilei Hao, and Bochu Wang, "Unraveling the Potential Human Health Risks from Used Disposable Face Mask-Derived Micro/Nanoplastics During the COVID-19 Pandemic Scenario: A Critical Review," *Environment International* 170 (2022): 107644, https://doi.org/10.1016/j.envint.2022.107644.

7. Mark Lieberman, "The Dismal State of School Infrastructure, in Charts," *Education Week*, April 27, 2021, https://www.edweek.org/leadership/the-dismal-state-of-school-infrastructure-in-charts/2021/04.

8. US Government Accountability Office, "K-12 Education: School Districts Frequently Identified Multiple Building Systems Needing Updates or Replacement," June 4, 2020, https://www.gao.gov/products/gao-20-494.

9. US Department of Education, *Frequently Asked Questions: Elementary and Secondary School Emergency Relief Programs—Governor's Emergency Education Relief Programs* (May 2021), https://www.ed.gov/media/document-2.

10. Department of Education, *Frequently Asked Questions.*

11. Austin Reed, "How Schools Are Spending Unprecedented Education Relief Funding," National Conference of State Legislatures, May 11, 2022, https://www.ncsl.org/state-legislatures-news/details/how-schools-are-spending-unprecedented-education-relief-funding.

12. Joseph Allen and Celine R. Gounder, "We Have a Once-in-a-Generation Opportunity to Fix Our Crumbling Schools," *The Hill*, October 8, 2021, https://thehill.com/opinion/education/577180-we-have-a-once-in-a-generation-opportunity-to-fix-our-crumbing-schools/.

13. Fionna Samuels, "Indoor Air Monitoring Goes to School," *Chemical & Engineering News*, August 30, 2024, https://cen.acs.org/analytical-chemistry/Indoor-air-monitoring-goes-school/102/i27.

14. *Merriam-Webster.com Dictionary*, s.v. "police power," accessed May 22, 2025, https://www.merriam-webster.com/dictionary/police%20power.

15. David E. Jacobs, Tom Kelly, and John Sobolewski, "Linking Public Health, Housing, and Indoor Environmental Policy: Successes and Challenges at Local and Federal Agencies in the United States," *Environmental Health Perspectives* 115, no. 6 (June 2007): 976–82, https://ehp.niehs.nih.gov/doi/10.1289/ehp.8990.

16. Megan Wallace and Joshua M. Sharfstein, "The Patchwork U.S. Public Health System," *New England Journal of Medicine* 386, no. 1 (January 6, 2022): 1–4.

17. Trust for America's Health, "The Impact of Chronic Underfunding on America's Public Health System: Trends, Risks, and Recommendations, 2023," June 14, 2023, https://www.tfah.org/report-details/funding-2023/.

18. I first saw the term "panic and neglect" in Ed Yong's articles about the COVID-19 response in *The Atlantic*.

19. Institute of Medicine (US) Committee for the Study of the Future of Public Health, *The Future of Public Health* (National Academies Press, 1988), https://www.ncbi.nlm.nih.gov/books/NBK218212/.

20. Apoorva Mandavilli, "The C.D.C. Isn't Publishing Large Portions of the Covid Data It Collects," *The New York Times*, February 22, 2022, https://www.nytimes.com/2022/02/20/health/covid-cdc-data.html.

21. Charles Piller, "Data Secrecy Is Crippling Attempts to Slow COVID-19's Spread in U.S., Epidemiologists Warn," *Science*, July 16, 2020, https://www.science.org/content/article/us-epidemiologists-say-data-secrecy-covid-19-cases-cripples-intervention-strategies.

22. Doug Donovan, "Schools Need Better Data to Grade COVID-19 Impact and Risk, Experts Say," Johns Hopkins University, September 20, 2021, https://hub.jhu.edu/2021/09/20/schools-covid-pandemic-data-initiative/.

23. S. E. Galaitsi, Jeffrey C. Cegan, Kaitlin Volk, Matthew Joyner, Benjamin D. Trump, and Igor Linkov, "The Challenges of Data Usage for the United States' COVID-19 Response," *International Journal of Information Management* 59 (2021): 102352, https://doi.org/10.1016/j.ijinfomgt.2021.102352.

24. Howard K. Koh, "We Need One Response—Not 50—to Fight Covid-19," *Stat*, May 22, 2020, https://www.statnews.com/2020/05/22/we-need-one-response-to-fight-covid-19-not-50/.

25. American Lung Association, *A National Asthma Public Policy Agenda—2022 Update* (May 2022), https://www.lung.org/getmedia/4c554601-a822-46f9-98aa-1bf6edc6782a/NatAsthmaPubPolAgenda2022Update.pdf.

26. American Lung Association, "Importance of Air Quality in Schools," accessed June 7, 2024, https://www.lung.org/clean-air/indoor-air/building-type-air-resources/at-school/importance-of-air-quality-in-schools.

27. Joseph Caputo, "School Meals Would Be Even Healthier If Compliant with U.S. Nutrition Standards, Study Finds," *Tufts Now*, July 31, 2023, https://now.tufts.edu/2023/07/31/school-meals-would-be-even-healthier-if-compliant-us-nutrition-standards-study-finds.

28. Maggie Davis, "State Efforts to Bolster Funding for Core Public Health Services," Association of State and Territorial Health Officials, October 25, 2024,

https://www.astho.org/communications/blog/state-efforts-to-bolster-funding
-for-core-public-health-services/.

CHAPTER 8

1. Regional Greenhouse Gas Initiative (RGGI), "A Brief History of RGGI," accessed September 13, 2024, https://www.rggi.org/program-overview-and-design/design-archive.
2. Regional Greenhouse Gas Initiative (RGGI), "About the Regional Greenhouse Gas Initiative," January 2025, https://www.rggi.org/sites/default/files/Uploads/Fact%20Sheets/RGGI_101_Factsheet.pdf.
3. Bruce R. Huber, "How Did RGGI Do It? Political Economy and Emissions Auctions," 40 *Ecology Law Quarterly* 59 (2013).
4. Huber, "How Did RGGI Do It?"
5. J. B. Wogan, "The Unlikely Comeback of Cap and Trade," *Governing*, January 23, 2018, https://www.governing.com/archive/gov-cap-and-trade-comeback-states.html.
6. Jonathan Ramseur, "The Regional Greenhouse Gas Initiative: Lessons Learned and Issues for Congress," *Congressional Research Service*, May 16, 2017, https://crsreports.congress.gov/product/pdf/R/R41836/14.
7. RGGI, "About."
8. Jingchi Yan, "The Impact of Climate Policy on Fossil Fuel Consumption: Evidence from the Regional Greenhouse Gas Initiative (RGGI)," *Energy Economics* 100 (2021): 105333, https://doi.org/10.1016/j.eneco.2021.105333.
9. Michelle Manion, Claire Zarakas, Stefanie Wnuck, Jacqueline Haskell, Anna Belova, David Cooley, et al., "The Regional Greenhouse Gas Initiative (RGGI) Analysis," Abt Associates, January 11, 2017, https://www.abtglobal.com/insights/publications/report/analysis-of-the-public-health-impacts-of-the-regional-greenhouse-gas.
10. Manion et al., "Regional Greenhouse Gas Initiative (RGGI) Analysis."
11. Manion et al., "Regional Greenhouse Gas Initiative (RGGI) Analysis."
12. Frederica Perera, David Cooley, Alique Berberian, David Mills, and Patrick Kinney, "Co-Benefits to Children's Health of the U.S. Regional Greenhouse Gas Initiative," *Environmental Health Perspectives* 128, no. 7 (July 2020), https://ehp.niehs.nih.gov/doi/10.1289/EHP6706.
13. Perera et al., "Co-Benefits to Children's Health."
14. Regional Greenhouse Gas Initiative (RGGI), *The Investment of RGGI Proceeds in 2022* (July 2024), https://www.rggi.org/sites/default/files/Uploads/Proceeds/RGGI_Proceeds_Report_2022.pdf.

15. Paul J. Hibbard, Susan F. Tierney, Pavel G. Darling, and Sarah Cullinan, "The Economic Impacts of the Regional Greenhouse Gas Initiative on Nine Northeast and Mid-Atlantic States," Analysis Group, April 17, 2018, https://www.ourenergypolicy.org/wp-content/uploads/2018/04/analysis_group_rggi_report_april_2018-3.pdf.

16. Juan Declet-Barreto and Andrew A. Rosenberg, "Environmental Justice and Power Plant Emissions in the Regional Greenhouse Gas Initiative States," *PLOS One* 17, no. 7 (2022): e0271026, https://doi.org/10.1371/journal.pone.0271026.

17. Barry G. Rabe, "The Complexities of Carbon Cap-and-Trade Policies: Early Lessons from the States," Brookings Institution, October 2008, https://www.brookings.edu/articles/the-complexities-of-carbon-cap-and-trade-policies-early-lessons-from-the-states/.

18. Rabe, "Complexities of Carbon Cap-and-Trade Policies."

19. Rabe, "Complexities of Carbon Cap-and-Trade Policies."

20. Huber, "How Did RGGI Do It?"

21. Wogan, "Unlikely Comeback."

22. Wogan, "Unlikely Comeback."

23. Barry Rabe, "Carbon Pricing Enters Middle Age," Wilson Center, June 8, 2023, https://www.wilsoncenter.org/article/carbon-pricing-enters-middle-age.

24. SERPPAS, "The Power of Unconventional Partnerships," accessed October 1, 2024, https://repi.osd.mil/portal/apps/storymaps/stories/d19228469f9e4ebb91f67e8a481af1ee.

25. SERPPAS, "About Us," accessed October 1, 2024, https://serppas.org/about-us.

26. SERPPAS, "Power."

27. The Nature Conservancy, "Red-Cockaded Woodpecker Wars," last updated May 14, 2024, https://www.nature.org/en-us/about-us/where-we-work/united-states/north-carolina/stories-in-north-carolina/red-cockaded-woodpecker-military-conservation/.

28. SERPPAS, "About Us."

29. SERPPAS, "Power."

30. "Department of the Interior, Fish and Wildlife Service: Reclassification of the Red-Cockaded Woodpecker from Endangered to Threatened with a Section 4(d) Rule," *Federal Register*, October 25, 2024, https://public-inspection.federalregister.gov/2024-23786.pdf.

31. SERPPAS, "Power."

32. SERPPAS, "Power."

33. SERPPAS, "Power."

34. The Nature Conservancy, "Red-Cockaded Woodpecker Wars."

35. Western Regional Partnership, accessed September 30, 2024, https://wrpinfo.org/.

36. Kenneth Olden, "The EPA: Time to Re-Invent Environmental Protection," *American Journal of Public Health* 108, no. 4 (April 2018), https://doi.org/10.2105/AJPH.2017.304303.

CHAPTER 9

1. Council on Education for Public Health, untitled table, accessed October 23, 2024, https://media.ceph.org/documents/D2_guidance.pdf.
2. Council on Education for Public Health, "CEPH Trends 2020: Environmental Health," accessed October 23, 2024, https://media.ceph.org/documents/Environmental_Health.pdf.
3. Carly R. Levy, Lynelle M. Phillips, Carolyn J. Murray, Lindsay A. Tallon, and Rosemary M. Caron, "Addressing Gaps in Public Health Education to Advance Environmental Justice: Time for Action," *American Journal of Public Health* 112, no. 1 (January 2022): 69–74, https://doi.org/10.2105/AJPH.2021.306560.
4. Karen Pennar, "Led by Students, a Nascent Climate Movement Is Taking Hold in Medical Education," *Stat*, April 26, 2023, https://www.statnews.com/2023/04/26/medical-education-climate-change-health-student-movement/.
5. Association for Prevention Teaching and Research, "Environmental Health Education," accessed August 12, 2024, https://www.aptrweb.org/page/EH_Education.
6. Deborah Heaney, "I'm a Doctor. Dengue Fever Took Even Me by Surprise on Vacation," *The New York Times*, April 3, 2024, https://www.nytimes.com/2024/04/03/opinion/dengue-fever-latin-america-travel.html.
7. US Centers for Disease Control and Prevention, "Environmental Public Health Tracking: About Funded Tracking Programs," accessed November 30, 2023, https://www.cdc.gov/environmental-health-tracking/php/our-work/index.html.
8. Mary A. Fox, Sheriza Baksh, Juleen Lam, and Beth Resnick, "Building the Future of Environmental Public Health Tracking: Proceedings and Recommendations of an Expert Panel Workshop," *Journal of Environmental Health* 79, no. 10 (June 2017): 14–19.
9. Massachusetts Office of Technical Assistance and Technology, Toxics Use Reduction Institute, and Department of Environmental Protection, *Annual Report Fiscal 2021—Massachusetts Toxics Use Reduction Program* (December 2022), https://www.mass.gov/doc/fiscal-year-2021-progress-report-on-the-massachusetts-toxics-use-reduction-program/download.
10. Toxics Use Reduction Institute, "Eliminating the Use of Toxic Chemicals in Dry Cleaning: A Cost Analysis of a Wet Cleaning Shop," accessed October 10, 2024, https://www.turi.org/publications/eliminating-the-use-oftoxicchemicals-in-dry cleaning/.

11. Polly Hoppin, Molly Jacobs, and Laurie Stillman, *Investing in Best Practices for Asthma: A Business Case for Education and Environmental Interventions* (Asthma Regional Council of New England, April 2007), https://nchh.org/resource-library/arc_investing-in-best-practices-for-asthma_a-business-case-for-education-and-environmental-interventions.pdf.

12. Elise Gould, "Childhood Lead Poisoning: Conservative Estimates of the Social and Economic Benefits of Lead Hazard Control," *Environmental Health Perspectives* 117, no. 7 (July 2009): 1162–67, https://doi.org/10.1289/ehp.0800408.

13. Fox et al., "Building the Future of Environmental Public Health Tracking."

14. Elizabeth Myers, "School IPM Pilot Projects Take Flight," Northeastern IPM Center, accessed August 22, 2024, https://www.northeastipm.org/about-us/publications/ipm-insights/school-ipm-pilot-projects-take-flight/.

15. Aplomb Consulting and Steadman Hill Consulting, Inc., "Memorandum: Rides to Wellness (R2W) Implementation Plan," April 4, 2018, http://vtrans.vermont.gov/sites/aot/files/publictransit/documents/Implementation%20Plan-Final.pdf.

16. San Francisco Environment Department, "Pest Management for City Departments," accessed August 12, 2024, https://www.sfenvironment.org/pest-management-for-city-departments.

17. Spencer Wagner, Nestor M. Davidson, Kim Haddow, Alex Jones, Christiana K. McFarland, and Brooks Rainwater, *Restoring City Rights in an Era of Preemption: A Municipal Action Guide* (National League of Cities, 2019), https://www.nlc.org/wp-content/uploads/2019/11/Restoring-City-Rights-in-an-Era-of-PreemptionWeb.pdf.

18. Public Health Law Program, "Preemption of Local Public Health Laws," accessed August 22, 2024, https://www.cdc.gov/phlp/docs/preemption-issue-brief.pdf.

19. Public Health Law Program, "Preemption of Local Public Health Laws."

20. Thomas A. Burke, Nadia M. Shalauta, Nga L. Tran, and Barry S. Stern, "The Environmental Web: A National Profile of the State Infrastructure for Environmental Health and Protection," *Journal of Public Health Management and Practice* 3, no. 2 (March 1997), https://www.jstor.org/stable/44967635.

21. Scott Burris, Laura Hitchcock, Jennifer Ibrahim, Matthew Penn, and Tara Ramanathan, "Policy Surveillance: A Vital Public Health Practice Comes of Age," *Journal of Health Politics, Policy and Law* 41, no. 6 (December 2016), https://doi.org/10.1215/03616878-3665931.

22. Burris et al., "Policy Surveillance."

23. Temple University Center for Public Health Law Research, "Policy Surveillance for Policymaking," May 14, 2019, accessed August 18, 2024, http://phlr.org/product/exploring-policy-surveillance-2019-webinar-series.

24. Temple University Center for Public Health Law Research, "Policy Surveillance for Policymaking."

25. Burris et al., "Policy Surveillance."
26. Scott Burris, Marice Ashe, Donna Levin, Matthew Penn, and Michelle Larkin, "A Transdisciplinary Approach to Public Health Law: The Emerging Practice of Legal Epidemiology," *Annual Review of Public Health* 37 (2016): 135–48, https://doi.org/10.1146/annurev-publhealth-032315-021841.
27. US Centers for Disease Control and Prevention, "Public Health Law: General Legal Epidemiology Competencies," May 15, 2024, https://www.cdc.gov/phlp /php/about/general-legal-epidemiology-competencies.html.
28. Burris et al., "Policy Surveillance."
29. American Medical Association, "Trends in Health Care Spending," accessed July 9, 2024, https://www.ama-assn.org/about/research/trends-health-care-spend ing.
30. Trust for America's Health, "The Impact of Chronic Underfunding on America's Public Health System 2024: Trends, Risks, and Recommendations," August 21, 2024, https://www.tfah.org/report-details/funding-2024/.
31. Trust for America's Health, "Impact of Chronic Underfunding."
32. Paul J. Fleming, Maren M. Spolum, William D. Lopez, and Sandro Galea, "The Public Health Funding Paradox: How Funding the Problem and Solution Impedes Public Health Progress," *Public Health Reports* 11, no. 136 (November 2020): 10–13, https://doi.org/10.1177/0033354920969172.
33. Trust for America's Health, "What If Congress Adequately Funded Public Health?," accessed October 15, 2024, https://www.tfah.org/story/what-if-con gress-adequately-funded-public-health/.

CHAPTER 10

1. Susan Kaplan, Susan Buchanan, and Debyante Porter Onduto, *Investigating Environmental Contamination: A Guide for Communities* (Great Lakes Center for Children's Environmental Health, University of Illinois Chicago School of Public Health, June 2019; updated April 2022), https://childrensenviro.uic.edu/wp -content/uploads/sites/812/2022/06/online_comm-resource-guide_03092020 -compressed-Final-w-Ethylene-compressed.pdf.
2. Kaplan et al., *Investigating Environmental Contamination.*
3. Vermont Department of Health, "Environmental Health Guide for Parents, Caregivers and Child Care Providers," last updated April 28, 2025, https://www .healthvermont.gov/environment/childrens-environmental-health/environmen tal-health-guide-parents-caregivers-and-child.
4. New Hampshire Department of Health and Human Services, "Children's Environmental Health Interactive Resource Guide," accessed May 24, 2025, https:

//www.dhhs.nh.gov/programs-services/environmental-health-and-you/environ
mental-public-health-tracking/childrens.

5. Council on Environmental Health, "Pesticide Exposure in Children," *Pediatrics* 130, no. 6 (December 2012): e1757–63, https://doi.org/10.1542/peds.2012-2757.

6. American Academy of Pediatrics, "Key Points About Pesticides," last updated January 11, 2024, https://www.aap.org/en/patient-care/environmental-health/promoting-healthy-environments-for-children/pesticides/.

7. Michael Hawthorne, "Lots of Smoke, Noise—But Not Much Action on Diesel Engine Idling," *Chicago Tribune*, August 19, 2019, https://www.chicagotribune.com/2010/11/21/lots-of-smoke-noise-but-not-much-action-on-diesel-engine-idling-3/.

8. Environmental Defense Fund, "Safer Chemicals, Healthy Families: Diverse Health and Environmental Coalition Calls for Sweeping Changes in U.S. Chemical Safety Law," Press Release, August 4, 2009, https://www.edf.org/media/safer-chemicals-healthy-families-diverse-health-and-environmental-coalition-calls-sweeping.

9. Joshua A. Basseches, Rebecca Bromley-Trujillo, Maxwell T. Boykoff, Trevor Culhane, Galen Hall, Noel Healy, et al., "Climate Policy Conflict in the U.S. States: A Critical Review and Way Forward," *Climatic Change* 170, no. 32 (2022), https://doi.org/10.1007/s10584-022-03319-w.

10. The Network for Public Health Law, *The State of State-Level Public Health Advocacy: Findings and Implications from a 50-State Scan* (October 2023), https://www.networkforphl.org/wp-content/uploads/2023/10/PH-Advocacy-Scan-Summary-Final-October-2023.pdf.

11. Amy Halpern-Laff, "Transcription of the Episode 'Paula Rogovin: Creating a Social Justice Early Childhood Classroom,'" *Ethical Schools*, October 30, 2019, https://ethicalschools.org/2019/10/transcription-of-the-episode-paula-rogovin-creating-a-social-justice-early-childhood-classroom/.

12. Halpern-Laff, "'Paula Rogovin.'"

13. Halpern-Laff, "'Paula Rogovin.'"

14. Ben Kallos, "Toxic Pesticides Ban in Parks Proposed by New York City Council Members Kallos and Rivera," Press Release, April 18, 2019, https://benkallos.com/press-release/toxic-pesticides-ban-parks-proposed-new-york-city-council-members-kallos-and-rivera.

15. Anne Barnard, "N.Y.C. Bans Pesticides in Parks with Push from Unlikely Force: Children," *The New York Times*, April 24, 2021.

16. Mount Sinai Health System, "Events: Involving Young Children in the Fight for Legislation to Ban Toxic Pesticides: Paula Rogovin," accessed November 15, 2024, https://events.mountsinaihealth.org/event/involving_young_children_in_the_fight_for_legislation_to_ban_toxic_pesticides_paula_rogovin.

17. The Black Institute, *Poison Parks* (January 2020), accessed November 15, 2024, https://theblackinstitute.org.
18. "Local Laws of the City of New York for the Year 2021: No. 56," accessed November 15, 2024, https://intro.nyc/local-laws/2021-56.
19. Kallos, "Toxic Pesticides Ban in Parks."
20. Beyond Pesticides, "On Earth Day, Coalition Calls on NYC Parks Department to Set Up Demonstration Sites," Press Release, April 20, 2022, https://www.beyondpesticides.org/resources/media/on-earth-day,-coalition-calls-on-nyc-parks-department-to-set-up-demonstration-sites.
21. Kallos, "Toxic Pesticides Ban in Parks."
22. Kaplan et al., *Investigating Environmental Contamination.*
23. Barnard, "N.Y.C. Bans Pesticides in Parks."
24. Parks for Kids NYC (@parksforkidsnyc), Facebook, accessed November 25, 2024, http://www.facebook.com/parksforkidsnyc.
25. Parks for Kids NYC (@parksforkidsnyc), Facebook, accessed November 25, 2024, http://www.facebook.com/parksforkidsnyc.
26. Parks for Kids NYC (@parksforkidsync), Facebook, accessed November 25, 2024, https://www.facebook.com/parksforkidsnyc.
27. Maida Galvez, Geoffrey Collins, Robert W. Amler, Allen Dozor, Evonne Kaplan-Liss, Joel Forman, et al., "Building New York State Centers of Excellence in Children's Environmental Health: A Replicable Model in a Time of Uncertainty," *American Journal of Public Health* 109 (2018): 108–12, https://doi.org/10.2105/AJPH.2018.304742.
28. Florida League of Cities, Inc., *2018 Executive Director's Annual Report* (n.d.), https://www.floridaleagueofcities.com/docs/default-source/pubs/2018-flc-annual-report-for-web.pdf.

CONCLUSION

1. Jacob Gerken, Gear Thomas Vincent, Demi Zapata, Ileana G. Barron, and Isain Zapata, "Comprehensive Assessment of Pesticide Use Patterns and Increased Cancer Risk," *Frontiers in Cancer Control and Society* 2 (July 24, 2024), Sec. Social Determinants in Cancer, https://doi.org/10.3389/fcacs.2024.1368086.
2. Charles Piller, "Data Secrecy Is Crippling Attempts to Slow COVID-19's Spread in U.S., Epidemiologists Warn," *Science*, July 16, 2020, https://www.science.org/content/article/us-epidemiologists-say-data-secrecy-covid-19-cases-cripples-intervention-strategies.
3. Austyn Gaffney, "A Climate Resistant Community Passed Two Hurricane Tests," *The New York Times*, October 15, 2024, https://www.nytimes.com/2024/10/15/climate/florida-climate-resilience-babcock-ranch.html.

4. Joseph Winters, "The 5 States Where Environmental Ballot Initiatives Triumphed," *Grist*, November 7, 2024, https://grist.org/politics/environment-con servation-climate-resilience-ballot-initaitives-election/.

5. Daniel Aldana Cohen and Thea Riofrancos, "Biden Left Us with a 'Prius Economy.' It's Time for Something Different," *The New York Times*, January 7, 2025, https://www.nytimes.com/2025/01/07/opinion/electric-vehicles-tax-credits .html.

6. Rebecca Raney, "Pesticide-Related PAC Money Surges into State Legislatures As Companies Seek to Limit Damage Awards in Court," *U.S. Right to Know*, October 31, 2024, https://usrtk.org/pesticides/pesticide-related-pac-money-surges -into-state-legislatures/.

SOURCES FOR FURTHER INFORMATION

ENVIRONMENTAL HEALTH POLICY

National Conference of State Legislatures
https://www.ncsl.org/
National Caucus of Environmental Legislators
https://ncelenviro.org/
American Public Health Association
https://www.apha.org/
Environmental Council of the States
https://www.ecos.org/

TOXICS USE REDUCTION/POLLUTION PREVENTION

Interstate Chemicals Clearinghouse
https://www.theic2.org/
US EPA: Pollution Prevention (P2)
https://www.epa.gov/p2
Change Chemistry
https://member.changechemistry.org/

INTEGRATED PEST MANAGEMENT

IPM Institute of North America
https://ipminstitute.org/
San Francisco Environment Department
https://www.sfenvironment.org/pest-management-for-city-departments
US EPA's Approach for IPM in Schools
https://www.epa.gov/ipm/epas-approach-integrated-pest-management-schools

ENVIRONMENTAL AND OCCUPATIONAL HEALTH EDUCATION

National Environmental Health Association
https://www.neha.org/
Association for Prevention Teaching and Research
https://www.aptrweb.org/
National Institute of Environmental Health Sciences: Environmental Health Science
    Education
https://www.niehs.nih.gov/health/scied
Mount Sinai Selikoff Centers for Occupational Health: Educational Resources
https://www.mountsinai.org/care/occupational-health/educational-resources
National Institute for Occupational Safety and Health: About the Total Worker
    Health Approach
https://www.cdc.gov/niosh/twh/about/?CDC_AAref_Val=https://www.cdc.gov
    /niosh/twh/totalhealth.html

CHILDREN'S ENVIRONMENTAL HEALTH

Pediatric Environmental Health Specialty Units
https://pehsu.net/
Children's Environmental Health Network
https://cehn.org/
American Academy of Pediatrics: Promoting Healthy Environments for Children
https://www.aap.org/en/patient-care/environmental-health/promoting-healthy-envi
    ronments-for-children

CUMULATIVE IMPACTS

US EPA: EJScreen: Environmental Justice Screening and Mapping Tool
https://screening-tools.com/epa-ejscreen
California Office of Environmental Health Hazard Assessment: CalEnviroScreen
https://oehha.ca.gov/calenviroscreen
California Air Resources Board: Community Air Protection Program Blueprint 2.0
https://ww2.arb.ca.gov/capp/resources/final-community-air-protection-blueprint
    -20-2023
PurpleAir
https://www2.purpleair.com/

HEALTH IN ALL POLICIES

Association of State and Territorial Health Officials
https://www.astho.org/
National Association of County and City Health Officials
https://www.naccho.org/
SOPHIA: The Community of HiAP Professionals
https://hiasociety.org/

COVID-19 MITIGATION IN SCHOOLS

Healthy Schools Network
https://healthyschools.org/
Harvard T.H. Chan School of Public Health: Healthy Buildings
https://www.hsph.harvard.edu/healthybuildings/
U.S. EPA Tools for Schools Resources
https://www.epa.gov/iaq-schools/iaq-tools-schools-resources

REGIONAL PACTS

Regional Greenhouse Gas Initiative
https://www.rggi.org/
Southeast Regional Partnership for Planning and Sustainability (SERPPAS)
https://serppas.org

PREEMPTION

National League of Cities: Restoring City Rights in an Era of Preemption: A Municipal Action Guide
https://www.nlc.org/wp-content/uploads/2019/11/Restoring-City-Rights-in-an-Era-of-PreemptionWeb.pdf
CDC Public Health Law Program: Preemption of Local Public Health Laws
https://www.cdc.gov/phlp/docs/preemption-issue-brief.pdf

LOCAL ACTION

ICLEI-Local Governments for Sustainability
https://iclei.org/

Urban Sustainability Directors Network
https://www.usdn.org/index.html#/
Institute for Sustainable Communities
https://sustain.org/
Big Cities Health Coalition
https://www.bigcitieshealth.org/
International City/County Management Association
https://icma.org

POLICY SURVEILLANCE AND LEGAL EPIDEMIOLOGY

LawAtlas
https://lawatlas.org/
Temple University Beasley School of Law: Policy Surveillance Program
https://phlr.temple.edu/
CDC: Public Health Law
https://www.cdc.gov/phlp/php/index.html
Network for Public Health Law
https://www.networkforphl.org/

Advocacy
American Public Health Association Policy Action Institute
https://www.apha.org/events-and-meetings/policy-action-institute
American Academy of Pediatrics: Advocacy
https://www.aap.org/en/advocacy/
American College of Obstetricians and Gynecologists: Advocate in Your State
https://www.acog.org/advocacy/abortion-is-essential/advocate-in-your-state

INDEX

Photo by David Block

ABOUT THE AUTHOR

Susan Kaplan, JD, is research assistant professor of Environmental & Occupational Health Sciences at the University of Illinois Chicago. She previously developed regulations at the Occupational Safety and Health Administration in Washington, DC, managed a state program to clean up and redevelop contaminated sites, and was assistant director of an energy policy group at Harvard University's Kennedy School. Her writing has appeared in *The Washington Post*, *Boston Globe*, *Christian Science Monitor*, *Ensia*, and other outlets.